The Fundamental 5

The Formula for Quality Instruction

Sean Cain & Mike Laird

ISBN: 1456491032
ISBN-13: 9781456491031

Dedications

I dedicate this book to the five educators who made the biggest impact on my education, career, and life: Ronald Maas (Aldine ISD), Betsy Shipper (Aldine ISD), Tommy Wallace (Aldine ISD), Roy Smith (Aldine ISD), and Richard Hooker (University of Houston). I stand on their shoulders.

S. Cain

I dedicate this book to the most important people in education today, classroom teachers. When all is said and done, it is the teachers who do the heavy lifting in education. What and how well they teach our children is critical to our future success as a society, and they deserve the best leadership and support that we can provide them.

M. Laird

Table of Contents

CHAPTER ONE

Introduction

The basic practices of quality instruction are not a secret. Observe a teacher providing instruction in a one-on-one setting and a teacher providing instruction to a packed lecture hall; one will recognize similar practices and strategies. Even the distinction between high-yield instructional practices, as identified by Marzano, Pickering, and Pollock (2001), and lower-yield instructional practices (such as lecture and worksheets) are fairly common and accepted—at least they are accepted on paper. However, in terms of individual pedagogy, the individual comfort level and preferences of the teacher often trump research, which leads to a critical observation: dramatically improving the quality of both individual and staff pedagogy is easy. In fact, it is as easy as losing weight. What this means is that the concept is simple, yet difficult to accomplish without a great deal of self-discipline.

Simple Is Not Always Easy

Everyone knows the secret to losing weight: just eat less and exercise more. In theory, it is a piece of cake. Oops, perhaps not the best analogy to use. Not losing weight is merely implementation failure at some critical juncture. Granted, this diet failure can have many causes, some of which include the following:

1. Not having a good plan—The "Eat Cupcakes and Lie on the Couch" diet and exercise plan may be easy to implement, but it is highly unlikely that the dieter will be ready for the upcoming swimsuit season.
2. Not having the desire—If one is satisfied with or indifferent to the current situation, then finding the internal motivation to change is at best slow and difficult.
3. Procrastination—(Authors' note*—Write about this point tomorrow).
4. Not recognizing the opportunity loss—Perhaps a two-day hiking trip in the mountains with one's family will be the most rewarding experience that the family might ever have together. However, one will never find out if one is not physically prepared enough to participate when the opportunity is presented.
5. Not having support—Temptation is everywhere. One falls into bad habits because they are easy, quick, and/or provide pleasure or short-term relief. Having people who are engaged in facilitating one's attempt to improve dramatically increases the chances of a successful outcome.

6. Not having a way to regularly and accurately gauge progress—If one does not have the processes and tools with which to gauge results, whether that is to regularly step on the scale, regularly track inches lost, or try on an older pair of pants, then it is hard to determine if the diet and exercise plan is working.

Now let us examine the other side of the diet-pedagogy analogy. The failure to dramatically and systematically improve classroom instruction follows the same pattern as the failure to successfully diet. Here are some reasons why efforts to improve classroom instruction fail.

1. Not having a good plan—The "Teach from the Desk and Distribute Worksheets" daily instructional plan is easy to implement. But as accountability standards increase, will student performance keep pace, or will it invariably decline, relative to the new standard?

2. Not having the desire—If one is satisfied or indifferent with the current level of student performance, then generating the internal motivation to change is slow and difficult.

3. Procrastination—(Authors' note*—Address this point next semester).

4. Not recognizing the opportunity loss—What is better for the student: attending a trade school or a community college? A community college or a state university? A state university or a private university?

A private university or an Ivy League school? Why should an individual teacher get to decide? Educators have a moral imperative to push and prepare every student to exceed expectations: theirs, ours, and the community's. Not all students will, but if schools and teachers do not do their part, no student will.

5. Not having support—Changing one's instructional practice is hard work. In the initial stages of change, one feels less comfortable and less effective. The easiest thing to do is to revert back to old practices. Having peers and leadership that are engaged in the same change process and working to facilitate each other's success dramatically increases the chances of that success.

6. Not having a way to regularly and accurately gauge progress—If one does not have a method to gauge results, the attempt to change will collapse under the weight of discomfort and perceived failure. Teachers need reliable short-term metrics to determine what is working and what is not and to make timely adjustments to their craft in order to successfully implement and complete the changes to their pedagogy. Two tools that assist with this and are within the means of any teacher and any campus are "short-term common assessments" and "PowerWalks" instructional data.[1]

---

1. PowerWalks: An electronic system that collects and disaggregates multiple short-term classroom observations for the specific purpose of collecting objective data on pedagogy as it is actually practiced. PowerWalks are neither content nor grade-level specific.

The Fundamental Five

At this point, the reader may ask, "Is there a simple plan for dramatically improving the effectiveness of classroom instruction?" The answer to this question is: Yes. There is a simple plan that any teacher can implement today that will begin to improve the quality of classroom instruction.

The plan identified by the authors is the high-frequency and high-quality execution of the "Fundamental Five." The Fundamental Five are the five critical practices that are at the core of highly effective instruction. These practices are:

1. Frame the Lesson
2. Work in the Power Zone
3. Frequent, Small-Group, Purposeful Talk about the Learning
4. Recognize and Reinforce
5. Write Critically

The Perfect Storm

The explanations of and strategies for implementing these five practices are at the heart of this book. However, a brief summary of their discovery is in order. In many ways, the identification of the Fundamental Five was the result of an educational "perfect storm." The storm began (for the authors) with a significant change to the school accountability standards in the state of Texas.

Changing Accountability Standards

First, Texas implemented the practice of assigning annual school (and district-level) ratings based on the lowest score achieved by any single set of disaggregated student groups, in any core subject area, on the annual state accountability test. In other words, a campus was only as good as its lowest-scoring disaggregated population of students based on state-selected criteria. This method eliminated the practice of averaging the scores of all students on campus: a practice that made small but unsuccessful groups of students invisible in the ratings. Districts and schools could no longer hide the fact that they were not meeting the needs of certain students.

While the "All Students" group was kept as one indicator, the additional disaggregated groups that were created and that impacted school ratings were: African American, Hispanic, White, Native American, Asian/Pacific Islander, economically disadvantaged, and students with special needs. It is important to understand that the accountability system is more complicated than this and contains other accountability measures and nuances. However, the move to focus on each disaggregated student population completely changed the way schools looked at data. The average passing rate of all the students on a given campus, from both an accountability standpoint and public perception, no longer mattered.

Second, Texas began to incrementally raise the minimum passing standard and minimum passing requirement of the accountability tests. These concepts are not the same. Essentially, the passing standard is the minimum required individual student score. The passing requirement is the minimum required percentage of students that must meet the passing standard. This meant that if a school maintained the status quo (the goal of many districts and campuses), in a short span of time, the annual rating of a campus could slide from exemplary to recognized, from recognized to academically acceptable, and from academically acceptable to academically unacceptable. Unfortunately, this is a slide that many Texas schools experienced and one that is currently being experienced in schools across the country as federal No Child Left Behind (NCLB) accountability practices and standards are implemented.

Accountability Changes the Game

What became evident in Texas, and what educators in schools across the country are also realizing under NCLB, is that doing nothing *overtly wrong* is no longer good enough. The requirement now is that teachers and schools have to do a number of things *significantly right* just to keep up with the ever-rising accountability bar.

Faced with this fundamental change in accountability standards, in the early 2000s, a small but significant number of schools began to aggressively attempt to improve student performance. These schools represented a fair and substantial cross section of Texas campuses. There were rural, suburban, and urban schools. There were small, medium, and large schools as well as poor, middle-class, and affluent schools. There were unacceptable, acceptable, recognized, and exemplary schools, and there were elementary, middle, high, and alternative schools. Essentially, these schools created a self-selected test group, with the other schools in the state becoming the control group. Over time, it became possible to observe the differences in performance that occurred between campuses that refused to change, campuses that grudgingly changed, and campuses that aggressively changed.

Around and during the same time (early 2000s), the education literature became more precise, directive, and prescriptive. For example, *Classroom Instruction that Works* (2001), by Marzano, Pickering, and Pollack, gave teachers specific practices to include in their delivery of instruction. Mike Schmoker, with his series of books culminating with *Results Now* (2006), focused on the theme of results and provided school leaders with an early blueprint on how to use short-term data to focus the practices and procedures of a campus on improved learning. Many of the aggressively changing campuses were attempting to implement, either formally or informally, the practices that were being described in these and similar works.

Cain's Foundation Trinity

The aggressively changing schools were early adopters of three fundamental practices that improved their instructional system. Those practices, identified by then State Director of Innovative School Redesign (Texas) Sean Cain, are:

1. The implementation of a common scope and sequence.
2. The use of short-term common assessments.

3. The increased monitoring and support of classroom teachers by campus instructional leadership and support personnel.

As then named by Cain, these practices are now regularly referred to as the Foundation Trinity. A campus that implements the Foundation Trinity provides its teachers with the luxury of focused time. When teachers do not have to spend significant time solving the problems of *what* to teach, *when* to teach it, and *how* to teach and assess it, they are able to focus their time and attention on what really matters. The Foundation Trinity allows teachers to concentrate their singular efforts on the "*how* to teach it" component, which improves the effectiveness of actual instruction.

Not only was Texas an early adopter of accountability standards, it was an early adopter in the collection of student, campus, and district performance data. Now there was a sudden influx of never-before-available anecdotal and empirical data. Student performance by disaggregated student subgroups could now be tracked over time and compared to both similar and dissimilar groups. Larger patterns could be identified. The instructional practices that produced both ends of the bell curve (of student performance) could be and were visited and studied, both informally and formally. This was a heady time for both the "data geek" and "practitioner" alike. If a person was both of these, it became the equivalent of working in a professional nirvana.

Key Support Providers

Add to the above mix two key support providers, E. Don Brown, a past president of the National Association of Secondary School Principals and one of the architects of *Breaking Ranks* (1996), and Sean Cain. The Texas commissioner of education assigned these two recognized school-improvement specialists the task of directly supporting a number of these aggressively improving campuses. Working hand in hand with multiple campuses and multiple contracted service providers, the team of Brown and Cain were actively searching for and identifying overriding trends and common elements that either accelerated or decelerated improvement efforts. Perhaps what was even more important than the formal roles that these two served was the informal role that they occupied, and this became critical to the "perfect storm." Brown and Cain became the de facto communication system for a statewide network of reform-minded schools, which was independent of a commercial agenda. The principals and schools in this network were no longer working, creating, and implementing in isolation; they were collectively sharing in the creation of new knowledge and a better understanding of how to rapidly improve all students' performance.

The Tipping Point

The above-described perfect storm reached a tipping point around 2005–2006. Without warning or an overt plan, a critical mass of practitioners began having lots of conversations on and about the same topic. In the effort to rapidly improve student performance, the overriding question became "What is working and why?"

The analysis of early anecdotal as well as empirical data made it clear that there were two ways to rapidly change the performance of a school. The first way was to change the composition of the student body. Students of wealth, in general, outperform students of poverty, and the research supports this fact. "In studies conducted from New York to New Mexico, scholars find that socio-economic status, English proficiency and cultural factors are major indicators of student success..." (Berliner 1990, 3). Additionally, Walberg and Fowler (1986, 1) state that "...numerous studies show that children from families of higher SES generally do better on achievement tests than children of lower SES." One would expect (at least theoretically) that when the relative wealth of neighborhoods served by a campus increases or decreases, there would be a corresponding change in student and campus academic performance. Therefore, improving the economic status of the student body should improve student performance. This can be done on a limited basis with magnet schools and theme-based schools. But at scale, this solution seems to merely reshuffle the "haves and the have-nots."

The second way to change student performance was to dramatically improve the quality of classroom instruction. Short of blind luck and/or blatant gerrymandering of campus attendance zones, the obvious solution for a campus is to improve instruction. In the opinion of the authors, this is the solution that holds the most promise and is the easiest (in relation to other solutions) to implement in grand scale.

Teacher Craft

The authors agree with Mike Schmoker when he writes, "…the single greatest determinate of learning is not socio-economic factors or funding levels. It is instruction" (2006, 7). Teacher craft is arguably the most critical component in student academic success. In order to stay ahead of the rapidly changing system of demands and student needs, teachers must have access to and use the most up-to-date tools of instruction. Furthermore, the authors firmly believe that the vast majority of teachers are diligent and hardworking individuals. Yet, given all of this, we also know that some teachers are much more effective than most teachers.

This is where the Fundamental Five comes into play. These are the five fundamental pedagogical elements that set the stage for quality instruction—every lesson, every day. These fundamental practices are within the means of every teacher. Fortunately, every teacher who has been in a classroom for longer than a week is aware of at least one, if not all, of these practices. However, what sets the great teacher apart from the average teacher is the consistent, high-frequency, and high-quality daily execution of the five practices as a unit.

What makes the Fundamental Five so incredibly powerful is the synergy that is created when these practices are executed, as a synchronized routine, at both high frequency and high quality. This body of practice improves the performance for every type, age, and group of student. The Fundamental Five may very well be the aspirin and Band-Aid of education; it makes everything a little bit better and is the first line of defense in preventative strategies. Properly executed, the Fundamental Five helps struggling students survive and compete in academic settings, thus addressing many Response to Intervention (RTI) Tier 1 concerns. At the same time, in the same classroom, the Fundamental Five positions academically stronger students to achieve at levels that were previously beyond the collective imagination of the profession. The explanation for both of these occurrences will be addressed in subsequent chapters.

CHAPTER TWO

Overview

The authors emphasize that the five fundamentals of effective instruction, hereafter to be referred to as the Fundamental Five, are not a list of recommendations from which one can pick and choose. Rather, they represent five individual practices that interact and interconnect in such a manner that their dramatic positive effect is dependent on their coordinated use within the scope of a single lesson. One must execute all five fundamentals. If even one is missing or performed in a haphazard (or cursory) manner, the self-reinforcing aspect of each is greatly diminished. They are very much like the fingers in a fist. If even one finger is broken, the fist will not be able to strike with any force.

The Weakness of Current Practice

One of the great disadvantages of current common instructional practice is that in the mind of the teacher, they actually reinforce the belief that poor performance is the fault of the student and the root of excellent performance is the teacher. After all, as the teacher, one has either presented the material with passion and creativity or dumbed the lesson down to the lowest classroom denominator. The latter practice is also known as "lowering expectations." The results are that some students do well and some students do not. The teacher is led to believe that some results are outside the span of the teacher's control. In the typical classroom, the teacher can be correct in that assumption. However, this is because the teacher is structuring and presenting the typical lesson in a fundamentally flawed manner. This ensures that student performance remains correlated to well-known educational variables, such as socioeconomic status and at-risk factors, instead of teacher craft. When used correctly, the Fundamental Five form the building blocks for creating a solid foundation for value-added instruction. Without this solid foundation, other practices and instructional strategies become, in effect, parlor tricks, which create the illusion of improved instruction without any significant change in student performance.

Time on Task

Another variable outside the teacher's control is time. While time on task is important, time itself is a finite variable. Well-intentioned administrators constantly struggle with the master schedule in an attempt to rearrange time in order to improve student achievement. Much effort has gone into the argument on the use of time. For example, which is superior, a seven-period day or an eight-period day? What about the constant back-and-forth between the alternating block (AB), versus the modified block, versus whatever else is out there? Unfortunately, providing teachers additional time to perform what is "fundamentally flawed instruction" only creates more "fundamentally flawed instruction," and the constant changes to the master schedule become an exercise in administrative futility. Though there have been some very creative attempts to use time more effectively, the outcome generally remains the same. So while time can certainly be used inefficiently, once the use of time is (basically) maximized, little improvement in student performance remains possible by continuing to tinker with master schedules. It is the belief of the authors that if a fundamentally sound manner of using time did exist, it would have already been discovered.

Action Research

The authors of this book are current practitioners involved in daily action research. They work in and with schools that are making serious efforts to rapidly improve student achievement. The instructional strategies and practices they advocate, they use in classrooms, training rooms, and conference halls, putting their sweat, passion, and reputations on the line. Though formal research is generally years behind the current state of practice, the initial data on the effect of the Fundamental Five is promising (see chapter 8, "New Beginnings").

The authors have observed and understand that the state of current practice is simultaneously both ahead of and behind the current state of educational research. Some practice is so new that the research community has not had an opportunity to formally analyze, measure, and evaluate the instructional practice in question. Other common in-structional practices are well behind effective practices that have been validated by research. The use of less effective practices in lieu of more effective practices represents the knowing/doing gap, or the gap between what one knows to do and what one actually does. This knowing/doing gap has been addressed by many, with just one example provided by Pfeffer and Sutton (2000) when they point out, "Why knowledge of what needs to be done frequently fails to re-sult in action or behavior consistent with that knowledge… we came to call this the knowing-doing problem—the chal-lenge of turning knowledge about how to enhance orga-nizational performance into actions consistent with that knowledge" (4).

Now is the time to close the knowing/doing gap between typical practice and the purposeful use of the Fundamental Five. The Fundamental Five are not a secret (just as how to lose weight is not a secret), and the authors do not claim to have invented these practices. What the authors have done is identified the synergy that develops when all five practices are practiced as an instructional routine. With this solid foundation of instructional fundamentals in place, all other instructional practices and strategies have their effective-ness magnified. The nabobs will claim that they are already doing these practices, but this is a claim without substance. Observations and objective data from over seventeen thou-sand classrooms (Cain, unpublished research, 2009) indicate that they are not. For example, the graph below represents the results from the initial, unannounced classroom obser-vations from 924 classrooms, on fifty-six campuses, in four separate school districts, conducted in the fall of 2009. The sample of classrooms includes all grade levels (kindergarten to twelfth grade) and the four core content areas (English/language arts, mathematics, science, and social studies).

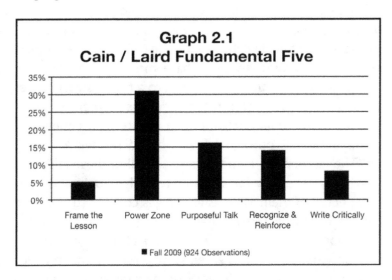

This graph illustrates the typical use of Fundamental Five practices by teachers on campuses where there has been little to no discussion, training, or support relating to these critical instructional practices. Sadly, based on the authors' observations of hundreds of campuses, this graph represents an accurate picture of the current state of instruction in public schools.

What Are the Fundamentals?

It is now appropriate to have a brief explanation and discussion of each of the Fundamental Five practices of effective instruction.

Framing the Lesson

Framing the lesson is a teacher practice that, as it is better implemented, is recognized as a quick fix to improve daily instruction. The practice, which is a written and verbal means of introducing the planned learning of the day, has evolved. Over time, teachers have moved from providing little prior information to students, to a broad statement of the teacher's intent, to a more specific statement (such as an agenda of student activities), to a statement couched in terms of learner outcomes (i.e., "The learner will know..." or "The learner will demonstrate..."). All of these fall short of what is necessary for students to truly understand what is expected of them as far as learning is concerned and their role in achieving the planned learning outcome. Current practitioners in the field need better and more specific advice on what constitutes an effective lesson frame in order to help maximize the efficiency of their instruction. The effective lesson frame provides the class with a clear picture of critical concepts that will be addressed by the lesson and the individual student with a clear picture of how he or she will demonstrate the understanding of the critical concepts.

Work in the Power Zone

Working in the power zone represents an improved understanding of the effect of teacher location on instructional outcomes. Changing teacher location in the classroom has generally been used as a noninstructional practice. The most widespread understanding of the use of teacher location is based on the notion of proximity control, that is, location viewed through the lens of student discipline and class-room management. For both of these, the teacher's location is a relevant and powerful concept. An even more powerful use of the practice is to view it through the lens of instructional delivery. Through that lens, teacher location becomes a fundamental element in improving student achievement and is a critical element in value-added instruction.

Frequent, Small-Group, Purposeful Talk about the Learning

The use of frequent, small-group, purposeful discussion on the academic topic is at least as old as Socrates and the Socratic method. It still represents one of the most effective instructional strategies that teachers use. When done, even in a mediocre manner, it provides the very real potential of shifting instruction to the higher levels of Bloom's taxonomy (1956)—analysis, synthesis, and evaluation. Unfortunately, even though the power and effectiveness of this strategy is well known, it is generally reserved for the most intrinsically motivated students and/or the most advanced courses. The use of meaningful discussion as a fundamental element does not rise to the level of an advanced Socratic seminar, nor even what currently passes for cooperative learning, but it does allow the most academically fragile students an opportunity to begin to develop the cognitive processes necessary to function at the highest levels of learning that it is surmised their future careers will require.

Recognize and Reinforce

Providing recognition and reinforcement addresses two sides of the learning coin, academics and behavior. Kotulak, in *Inside the Brain* (1997), points out that "children need to have their developmental advances recognized and praised. Positive feedback tells them their accomplishments are important…" (54).

Among the most powerful tools that teachers possess are the words they choose to use. Those words can be used to motivate students and build self-confidence or destroy students' self-image. They can make it possible for students to exceed their own internal limits or eliminate forever the students' willingness to attempt something that they might view as difficult or impossible. In the nonacademic world, there is an almost intuitive understanding of this. This is why spectators at a race gather at the finish line and scream encouragement to the runners so that they do not falter short of the finish line. Yet the academic world allows debate on the value of praise and reinforcement.

Write Critically

Writing critically is generally accepted as a valuable educational best practice. Ted Sizer (as cited in Schmoker 2006, 61) states, "Writing is the litmus paper of thought…the very center of schooling." Paul and Elder (2007, 4) state, "Writing is essential to learning. One cannot be educated and yet unable to communicate one's ideas in written form." But in the field, one observes two seemingly paradoxical facts. The first is that critical writing is a meaningful part of learning.

For students, critical writing creates meaning, solidifies connections, transforms subconscious ideas into conscious thoughts, and is essential for authentic literacy. "Generous amounts of close purposeful reading, writing, and talking… are the essence of authentic literacy. These simple activities are the foundation of a trained, powerful mind—and a promising future" (Schmoker 2006, 53). The second fact is that critical writing is unequivocally not part of the typical educational landscape. One could even argue that most educators seem to aggressively avoid introducing the practice in their classrooms. After a review of over seventeen thousand classroom observations during the 2008/2009 school year, critical writing was observed less than 10 percent of the time (Cain, unpublished research, 2009). This included thousands of observations in reading, writing, and secondary-level English/language arts classrooms where one would expect to observe a significant number of students writing critically. Even in these classrooms, this was not the case.

Summary and Justification

The authors believe that there are many reasons why these five practices are effective. The Fundamental Five work because they improve the focus of both the students and the teachers on the learning objective for every class. Conversation and critical writing improve both the students' understanding of the subject and their recall of the facts and concepts involved, as well as providing additional opportunities for teachers to increase the rigor of their lesson. The Fundamental Five assist in building student self-confidence and support for teachers as they build and improve appropriate academic relationships with their students. The Fundamental Five provide the teacher accurate, effective, and efficient feedback on the actual state of current student understanding. This ongoing, improved feedback allows the teacher to make constant microadjustments to instruction. This improved feedback is indicative of the entire class as opposed to the typical instructional feedback provided by the two or three best and/or most motivated students. These are the students who normally respond to teacher questions addressed to the entire group and provide the teacher with what is, in effect, a false positive on the true nature of current student understanding within the entire class. Finally, it is the routine use of these fundamental practices that improves the academic performance of the entire range of students. No single step is more or less important than the other, and it is the synergy of all five that, day in and day out, add value for the struggling student, the average student, and the high-performing student.

CHAPTER THREE

Framing the Lesson

What is a lesson frame? At its simplest level, a lesson frame represents the beginning and end of a lesson. Executed effectively, it becomes a powerful instructional resource. A lesson frame is made up of two distinct parts. The first part is the daily learning objective. It is a statement of what the student can expect to learn, today. The second part is the closing question, product, or task. The closing question, product, or task clearly states how the student will demonstrate his or her understanding of the learning objective for that day. In other words, the required student answer, product, or completed task serves as proof to both the teacher and the student that learning has taken place.

Essential Elements

Stating the learning objective at the very beginning of a lesson (or instructional unit within a larger lesson) must be a deliberate act on the part of the teacher. This objective generally addresses just a single day of instruction. What distinguishes a "lesson frame" objective from objectives as they are typically written is that the lesson frame objective is written in concrete, student-friendly language and is presented in the form of a "We will..." statement. For example:

> *"We will identify the components of an effective*
> *lesson frame."*

This statement is both simple and direct. The objective communicates to the student a clear focus for today's class.

The closing question, product, or task is also written in concrete, student-friendly language. It provides the student with a clear understanding of how he or she will demonstrate what was learned during the lesson. The demonstration of student understanding serves as the conclusion of the class. This provides proof to both the student and the teacher that the objective of the lesson was met. The closing question, product, or task is generally presented as an "I will..." statement. For example:

> *"I will create and share a lesson frame with my*
> *table group."*

Remember that a properly constructed lesson frame has two parts, and together, when crafted correctly, they improve the rigor of the lesson. As one will note from this example of a complete lesson frame:

*"We will identify the components of an effective
lesson frame."*
And,
"I will create and share a lesson frame with my table group."

Note how the teacher is able to deliberately move the students to higher levels of cognition by stretching the rigor between the objective and closing question, product, or task. The example objective is written at the comprehension level (key verb: *identify*) of Bloom's taxonomy. Successful completion of the example closing product will require student cognition at an even higher level of rigor, synthesis (key verb: *create*). Once developed, the lesson frame should be posted prominently in the classroom, such that it is visible and legible from anywhere in the classroom and so both the teacher and the student can refer back to it throughout the lesson.

Actual Examples of Elementary Classroom Lesson Frames

Language Arts (Elementary)

Objective:	We will identify the rising action in a work of fiction.
Closing Task:	I will work with a partner to identify and list words that create suspense.

Mathematics (Elementary)

Objective:	We will add and subtract decimals.
Closing Task:	I will compute the balance for my teacher's bank account.

Science (Elementary)

Objective:	We will identify natural sources of fresh water.
Closing Task:	I will complete an exit ticket describing the difference between fresh and salt water.

Social Studies (Elementary)

Objective:	We will discuss the regions of Texas and the products from each region.
Closing Task:	I will identify the most valuable region of Texas and justify my answer.

Actual Examples of Secondary Classroom Lesson Frames

Language Arts (Secondary)

Objective:	We will identify and discuss the themes of Macbeth.
Closing Task:	I will share with my partner which of the Macbeth themes apply in my life and why.

Mathematics (Secondary)

Objective:	We will identify the elements of line equations.
Closing Task:	I will write down how I would explain slope to a family member.

Science (Secondary)

Objective:	We will review lab safety practices and procedures.
Closing Task:	I will create a lab safety mnemonic with my lab partners and share it with the class.

Social Studies (Secondary)

Objective:	We will identify and discuss why two important battles became the turning point of the Civil War.
Closing Task:	I will be able to explain why a newspaper would write, "The South Will Lose the War," after these two battles.

Instructional Filters

Students are bombarded with a constant stream of information that they must rapidly sort, categorize, evaluate, prioritize, and make decisions about based on what is and is not important. In effect, the mind constantly filters new information in its effort to place the information in its proper place. Research indicates that an individual's working memory is limited in what it can track, and so it acts as a sort of spam filter (McCollough and Vogel 2008). The brain uses these mental filters to determine what to keep and what to discard. One keeps what one thinks is the more important information based on the specifics of the task (i.e., the teacher says, "Students, focus on the red tiles and ignore the rest for now") or, in the absence of being told what to ignore, by trying to link the task to preexisting schemas, or mental hooks, on which one can attach the newly presented content. In a classroom setting, the effectiveness of individual student mental filters can vary widely. From a content perspective, the effectiveness of mental filters is impacted by such variables as prior academic knowledge, prior academic success, enriched and varied life experiences, motivation, and level of stress, just to name a few.

One way to picture the mental filtering process is to think of a classroom with only two students. As the teacher presents the content to both students, one student has some useful mental filters relating to the content. This student can sort the new information into different categories—very useful, possibly useful, and not very useful. With this ability to sort and prioritize information, the student can better track with the teacher and do so for longer periods of time.

The other student has few and/or ineffective mental filters (as they relate to the content). For this student, there is only one category into which to sort the new information: very important. The problem with this is that if everything is equally important, it does not take long for the flow of information to overwhelm the learner. At some point, he or she reaches his or her capacity to process and retain any new information. This is information overload, and when this occurs, the learner is unable to continue tracking with the teacher and learning effectively stops. As one might surmise, possessing additional and more effective mental filters, as they relate to the content, provide a significant learning advantage.

The Socioeconomic Factor

Which students possess this learning advantage of prior academic knowledge, prior academic success, and enriched and varied life experiences? In general, these are the more affluent students in a given classroom. This helps explain why socioeconomic status is such a strong predictor of student performance. Students from the higher socioeconomic strata (in general) have had a much more enriched childhood than their less affluent peers. They have been read to, talked to, taken places, allowed to play with numerous and more varied toys, etc. They have been exposed to other children who also had an advantage in early life experiences, and thus even their playmates provide additional opportunities to improve existing learning filters or create new ones. The end result is that their life experiences have given them additional filters that impoverished students lack.

These initial life experience filters allow the student to follow the teacher more intently, and for longer periods of time, which speeds up the process of developing academic-based mental filters. This helps explain why—and data support—that students from a higher socioeconomic status have a clear advantage in academic settings and that poverty is known to have a depressing effect on student achievement (O'Hare 1988).

So how does framing the lesson address this concept of mental filters? It does so in the following way. For the student with weak, ineffective, or nonexistent content-related mental filters, the lesson frame serves in its place. When the teacher tells the class, "This is what we will learn today, and this is how you specifically will demonstrate that you learned it," the student can now begin sorting the presented content. The student can process the information in the following manner: this will help me demonstrate; this might help me demonstrate; this is not needed to demonstrate. Using this process, the student can now track with the teacher more effectively and for longer periods of time. Because the lesson frame serves as an external mental filter, it is important that the teacher post it prominently in the classroom and that it remain posted throughout the class period so students can refer to it as needed. The lesson frame is equally helpful to the student with some preexisting mental filters, as it relates to the content. In all likelihood, the preexisting mental filters are more general in nature. The lesson frame provides a filter that is focused on the critical learning for the day. This allows the higher-functioning student to substitute a useful tool with a more effective tool. The end result is not that learning took place, which in this case would have occurred even without the lesson frame, but that higher levels of learning took place, which then sets the stage for subsequent higher levels of learning. Thus, in terms of student performance, the regular and effective use of lesson frames has the very real potential of raising both the floor and ceiling performance levels of a given classroom.

Teacher Benefits

An effectively framed lesson provides the teacher with a clear and concise statement of the original intent of the lesson design. All subsequent instructional decisions should be made in light of that original intent. Once the teacher is clear on what concept(s) will be taught and how the student will demonstrate that he or she has learned that concept at the end of the lesson, the process of planning the lesson is significantly streamlined. The teacher simply selects the activities that will move students from the objective to the closing question, product, or task in an effective and efficient manner.

A prominently displayed lesson frame often assists teachers during the actual delivery of instruction. Consider the "teachable moment." The authors are firmly convinced that the reality is that these "moments" are, first, much less frequent than one would want to believe. Second, when these teachable moments do occur, they are much less valuable than the profession claims. Finally, these teachable moments rarely benefit the full range of students present in the classroom. As such, the visible lesson frame reduces the temptation to chase the teachable moment and stray from the original purpose of the lesson. If the teachable moment is valid, the lesson frame serves as a reminder to overtly tie the teachable moment back to the lesson frame, and hence the overriding intent of the day's instruction.

Students remember instructional content better if they find the material more relevant. Relevance helps make the content "sticky." For those who require a quick synopsis of instructional relevance, the education consultant group Lead Your School divides instructional relevance into three categories. The first instructional relevance category is "in-content." In-content relevance is the use of content-specific knowledge within the content area. For example, a student using acquired math skills to solve math problems in a math class would be an example of the in-content level of relevance. The second instructional relevance category is "across-content." Across-content relevance is the use of content knowledge or information from one content area to complete tasks in a different content area. For example, a student using math skills to better understand social studies concepts in a social studies class would be an example of the across-content level of relevance. The final instructional relevance category is "real-world." Real-world relevance is the use of content-specific knowledge to solve issues that directly relate to the student's nonacademic world. For example, a student using math skills to develop a budget for a holiday gift list would be an example of the real-world level of instructional relevance.

H. Lynn Ericson, in *Concept-Based Curriculum and Instruction* (2002), points out the need for standards-based curriculum to provide instructional relevance. She writes, "Although definitional knowledge of key concepts is critical, the focus for teaching and learning should be the essential ideas and understandings that incorporate the individual concepts. This brings relevance to the concepts" (26). However, even with a well-written, standards-based curriculum, the actual instructional decisions are still the responsibility of the teacher. Yet, many teachers struggle as they try to create and deliver lessons that reflect the understanding of the need for higher levels of relevance in their lessons. Given that teachers instruct many different students, sometimes as many as two hundred or more at the secondary level, the task of finding relevance for all students becomes exceedingly difficult. The authors have observed that in many cases, a properly framed lesson allows the students to create relevance for themselves and their fellow students. This student-created relevance is often different from what the teacher would have developed but is completely valid and effective in the eyes of the student. For example, consider the elementary math teacher who is teaching students how to distinguish between geometric shapes. The objective of the lesson could be:

"We will learn how to identify triangles and squares."

To complete the lesson frame, the teacher could use the following closing task:

"I will write down how triangles and squares are different."

Taken together, the lesson frame would look like this:

"We will learn how to identify triangles and squares."
And,
"I will write down how triangles and squares are different."

This would be a completely acceptable closing task. The rigor level of the lesson could be as high as analysis. But from a relevance standpoint, the answer to the question resides squarely in the content area. However, by selecting a different closing question, product, or task, the teacher can shift the area of relevance. For example:

"I will explain to my group some ways that triangles and squares are used in my home."

With this activity, the student must visualize his or her home and mentally check to see where the mathematical concept applies and does not apply. This act, driven by the lesson frame, increases the relevance level of the overall lesson as the content objective of identifying triangles and squares is extended from the classroom to the real-world setting of the student's home.

A properly framed lesson is also useful when it comes to providing the teacher with classroom observation feedback. Consider the observer, such as an administrator or an instructional coach, who visits a classroom that does not have a posted lesson frame. In the best-case scenario, the observer can tell the teacher that he or she was using some effective practices and that the students seemed to be engaged. This would be positive feedback, but not altogether useful feedback. On the other hand, if that same teacher had a lesson frame prominently displayed, the observer could improve the quality of the feedback provided to the teacher. Now, in addition to the information relating to teacher craft and student engagement, the observer can provide specific commentary on the most telling, yet often overlooked, piece of classroom observation data. Simply, does the observed classroom activity correlate to the teacher's planned intent, as evidenced by the lesson frame, or not? If the activity aligns, that is good information. If it does not, that is even better information, as classroom activity not aligned to the lesson frame generally represents misspent teacher and student effort. In the authors' opinion, it is the identification and realignment of this misspent effort that represents a critical first step in rapidly improving student performance.

The posted lesson frame helps keep all instructional decisions focused in light of the teacher's original intent, helps provide relevance, and serves as a constant point around which all other planning decisions can be made. As much as anything else, effective instruction is about decision making. Anything that can be done to improve teachers' initial and ongoing decision making is a positive, and a properly framed lesson helps accomplish that goal.

Student Benefits

A properly framed lesson also benefits students in several ways. First and foremost, it provides a visual cue and ongoing reminder to students of exactly what they are expected to know and do. This helps reduce or eliminate the all-too-typical practice of students having to guess or infer the purpose of the lesson, a practice that becomes increasingly difficult when the student is considered at risk. The lesson frame also provides an initial answer to the time-honored questions of *"Why do I need to know this?"* and *"When will I ever use this?"*

As a cognitive teaching tool, the lesson frame is of significant value in the classroom, as it supports and augments the use of mental filters. Mental filters represent the strategies and processes one uses to sort and process information. As mentioned previously, prior knowledge, prior experience, prior academic success, and motivation are just some of the components that enhance mental filters. Students with high-functioning mental filters are able to process information effectively and follow the lesson for longer periods of time before becoming confused and/or frustrated. Students with weaker mental filters struggle to process new information and can quickly become confused, frustrated, and, in extreme cases, noncompliant and belligerent.

When the teacher provides the class with a prominently displayed, student-friendly lesson frame, and then discusses said lesson frame with the class, the teacher is providing the students a filter with which to sort the information that is presented and discussed in class. A student with a weak mental filter (as it relates to the content) now has an additional way to sort and process information. Information that helps a student address the closing question, product, or task receives significant attention. Information that does little to address the closing question, product, or task is filtered to receive less attention. The practice of framing the lesson supports students with effective mental filters (as it relates to the content). As the content expert, the teacher-created lesson frame pinpoints for the advanced student the information that is critical to the day's learning activity. Thus the lesson frame provides the struggling student with a tool that makes it possible to keep pace with classroom demands, and the advanced student is provided an improved filter to better focus his or her thinking.

There is a final benefit to a prominently displayed, student-friendly lesson frame that is worth mentioning. As the practice becomes a classroom routine, it serves to support both distracted students and students who arrive late for class. Both of these groups of students learn to check the lesson frame in order to quickly integrate themselves into the learning activity, thus making the entire classroom more productive.

Putting It All Together

When developing a lesson frame, many teachers find the following process to be helpful.

1. Based on the curriculum source (for example, scope and sequence, textbook, etc.), the teacher determines the critical concept that students must understand for the lesson to be considered successful.
2. The teacher translates the critical concept into the age-appropriate language of the students who will be taught. This is the objective component of the lesson frame.
3. The teacher determines how the student can best demonstrate or prove that he or she understands the critical concept that is to be taught. The student should be able to demonstrate this critical understanding during the last five minutes of the class.
4. The teacher translates this student demonstration or proof into the age-appropriate language of the

student who will be taught. This is the closing question, product, or task component of the lesson frame.

When developing their lesson frames, teachers are encouraged to channel their inner Dr. Seuss and, in a clear and simple manner, just tell students, "Oh, the things we will learn today," and "Oh, the ways you will show me that you learned it."

Finally, as the staff of one school so poetically described it, a great lesson frame is like an Oreo cookie. One cookie is the concrete, student-friendly learning objective. One cookie is the closing question, product, or task. The yummy, creamy filling is all of the great instruction that brings it all together. Without all three components, one does not have an Oreo cookie. With all three, just add milk.

CHAPTER FOUR

Work in the Power Zone

Working in the power zone is perhaps the simplest of the Fundamental Five practices. To better understand this concept, consider the typical classroom when students are present. In the typical classroom, there are essentially three locations where a teacher can conduct his or her craft. The following is a presentation of these three locations, in order from least effective to most effective.

The Teacher Work Area

The first location where one could find a teacher is described as the teacher work area. The teacher work area is typically (but not always) the teacher's desk or computer nook. When in the teacher work area, the teacher is generally engaged in one of three common activities. The first activity is teacher "administrivia," which includes such tasks as checking roll, entering lunch counts, grading assignments, entering grades, checking e-mail, etc.

The second teacher work area activity commonly observed is no activity. The teacher is simply waiting for something to occur. The students are doing their assignments, getting or putting up supplies, grouping/dispersing, or engaging in other normal classroom activities, and the teacher is simply waiting in order to begin or continue instruction.

The third teacher work area activity commonly observed is the teacher delivering instruction from his or her desk. It is the authors' belief that the instructor work area is the least effective location in the classroom for a teacher to conduct his or her craft. It is an unfortunate reality that in many secondary classrooms, more instruction is delivered from the teacher work area than any other area of the classroom (Cain, unpublished research, 2009). The picture below is an illustration of the teacher work area. The star represents the teacher and the desks represent students.

Teacher Work Area

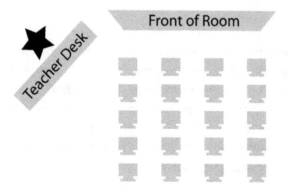

The Lecture Position

The second location where one typically observes teachers while students are in the classroom is what the authors refer to as the lecture position. When the teacher is occupying the lecture position, he or she is typically standing at the front of the room, the side of the room, or occasionally the back of the room.

The critical distinguishing factor that identifies the lecture position is a gulf, or purposeful space, between the students and the teacher. The teacher occupying the lecture position serves as the "sage on the stage," maintaining an appropriate but aloof professional distance. The students serve as the adoring audience, receiving information and taking notes—or perhaps being unbelievably bored but, if talented, pretending to be interested. When observing a class where the teacher primarily instructs from the lecture position, one is reminded of the classroom scenes in the classic *Peanuts* cartoons, by Charles Schultz. The students sit in quiet rows, trying to follow, while the teacher's drone of "Wah, wah-blah, wah" filters overhead. From an instructional delivery standpoint, the lecture position is generally more effective than teaching from the work area (i.e., the desk), but it is still not the most effective place for the teacher to work if student learning is the most important and desirable outcome. The pictures below are illustrations of the lecture position. The star represents the teacher and the desks represent students.

Lecture Position #1

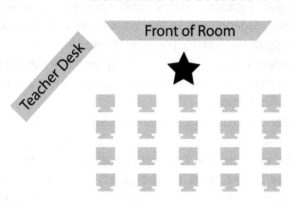

Lecture Position #2

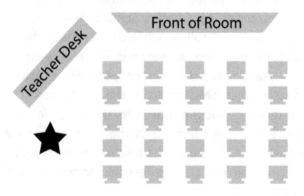

The Power Zone

It is the authors' position that when students are present in the classroom, the most effective place for a teacher to conduct his or her craft is what is described as the "power zone." A teacher occupying the power zone is simply teaching or monitoring in close proximity to one student, or a small group of students, or the entire classroom full of students. This proximity teaching or monitoring is referred to as "working in the power zone," because when a teacher engages in this practice, every other instructional practice that he or she brings to bear is enhanced and made more powerful.

When teachers conduct their practice in the power zone, a number of significant changes occur in the classroom dynamic. On-task behaviors increase, discipline issues decrease, and student retention of the content increases. When these variables are moving in the direction noted, there are generally corresponding increases in student achievement. The pictures below are illustrations of the power zone. The star represents the teacher and the desks represent students.

Power Zone #1

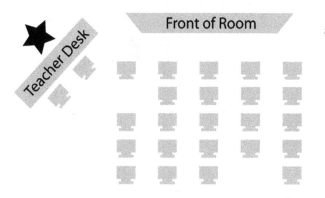

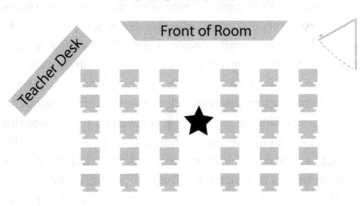

Proximity Instruction

The effect of proximity instruction on student behavior and performance should be of no surprise to most classroom teachers. After all, the concept of proximity instruction, with its roots in one-to-one tutoring, special education support, classroom management strategies, and discipline modification practices, is not new. However, what a small group of teachers were able to discover (either intuitively or through conscious action) was that when one engages in this practice all of the time, with every student, everyone in the class benefits.

Why is proximity instruction effective? There are a host of reasons, but perhaps most important, when teachers are in the power zone, they position themselves right in the middle of the action. When one is "in the fray," so to speak, one can easily identify and respond to minute changes in student performance and/or behavior. Now the teacher can reinforce positive behaviors that might otherwise be unnoticed, or, alternatively, extinguish negative behaviors before they reach a crisis stage. While in the power zone, the teacher is in the absolute best position to conduct frequent and ongoing formative assessment that allows the teacher to perform continuous microadjustments to instruction that are based on instantly identified student need. It is this microadjustment that allows tremendous increases in the effectiveness of instruction, which is a critical precursor to the improvement of student academic performance.

For a better understanding of this process, consider the simple act of adding and subtracting decimals. There is essentially one way to do this correctly. In order to be successful, the student has to line up the decimals, use the right operation, carry or borrow correctly, and know basic math facts. However, there are multiple ways to incorrectly execute this process. It behooves the teacher to quickly and accurately analyze exactly which misconception, which "wrong" way, the student is attempting to use to solve a problem, in order to provide appropriate corrective instruction. Otherwise, the teacher who addresses the wrong student misconception is often wasting both his or her own and the student's time and energy. The teacher who spends a significant amount of instructional time in the power zone is better able to accurately address specific student misconceptions, which increases student success and, in many cases, increases the overall pace of instruction, allowing teachers to increase the depth and/or breadth of the content presented, hence the term "power zone."

Putting It All Together

In discussions with teachers who spend a significant amount of instructional time in the power zone, the following suggestions are commonly shared.

1. Make a conscious commitment to the practice. The teachers who purposely seek out the power zone are able to remain in close proximity to one or more students in excess of 75 percent of a given class period (Cain, unpublished research, 2009).

2. Purposefully arrange the classroom to facilitate teacher movement. In crowded classrooms, this

often requires the teacher to sacrifice furnishings and storage areas to create more room for movement.

3. Limit or remove common teacher distractions. For example, the teacher may turn off his or her computer to remove the temptation to read or respond to e-mail. Or the teacher can commit to keeping a clean and organized desk, so as not to be tempted to do common paperwork while students are in the classroom.

Until recently, a teacher's use of the power zone has been looked at through the lens of classroom management and student behavior modification, and rightfully so, because it is a successful strategy for those purposes. But through that lens, working in the power zone is only a strategy. However, when viewed through the lens of instruction, this strategy becomes a fundamental practice. A teacher who increases time spent in the power zone improves classroom management, but, more importantly, he or she is in the position to improve classroom productivity and increase student performance. The authors' challenge to teachers when they train them on the power zone concept is this:

"If one is going to expend considerable time and energy to plan a lesson; if one is going to expend considerable time and energy to teach the lesson; if one is going to expend considerable time and energy to assess the lesson; and, ultimately, if one is evaluated on the effectiveness of the lesson; why wouldn't one position oneself in the location that will produce the best results?"

Stories from the Field

During the course of a Fundamental Five training session, an assistant principal shared the following story with the authors:

I sent an e-mail to my teachers during the middle of a class period. I almost immediately received a response from one teacher, to which I replied, "Why are you answering my e-mail during class?"

To which she replied, "Why did you send me an e-mail that required a response during class?"

At that moment, I realized that I have to do my part to help my teachers stay in the power zone. Now I only send my teachers e-mail before or after school.

CHAPTER FIVE

Frequent, Small-Group, Purposeful Talk about the Learning

The fundamental practice of frequent, small-group, purposeful talk about the learning (FSGPT) is perhaps the most self-explanatory of the Fundamental Five practices, yet it still requires explanation. It is the practice where, after every ten to fifteen minutes of teacher-driven discussion, or at the completion of a major instructional concept (whichever comes first), the teacher briefly stops talking and has groups of two to four students (hence the term *small group*) briefly discuss a seed question related to the instruction or the instructional activity. Keep in mind this is not a long conversation, nor is it an unstructured one. It is a focused microdiscussion lasting between thirty seconds and three minutes, with the structure for this fundamental practice provided by the teacher in four ways. This structure is made up of frequency, the group size, the seed question, and the power zone.

Frequency

The FSGPT structural component of frequency is created when the teacher plans for, allows, and then manages regular student discussions. Again, the rule of thumb is to provide for student discussion after every ten to fifteen minutes of teacher talk. This gives the students the opportunity to briefly discuss what they have learned. The power of these discussions will be covered in the ensuing paragraphs of this chapter.

Group Size

Group size makes up one of the FSGPT structural components. The teacher simply groups students in groups of two to four. Two students is, of course, the minimum size of a group, due to the fact that it requires at least two people to have a conversation, but note that the maximum recommended group size is four students. When more than four students are in a group, the teacher introduces two potentially disadvantageous variables. With five or more students, it is possible for a student to not participate in the discussion and no one will notice. The second disadvantage is that with five or more students, the possibility of side conversations being introduced within the group becomes increasingly likely, and few of these side conversations meet the instructional intent of the teacher.

Seed Question

The third structural component of FSGPT is the practice of using preplanned seed questions. The purpose of these questions is to guide the student conversations toward the desired learning outcome. This ensures that students are in the position to better make the connections that are critical to the content being presented. For example, after ten minutes of instruction, the teacher stops and gives the following directions: "Now I want you to briefly discuss with your partner the difference between the English monarchy and the American presidency" or "Discuss with your partner(s) the… (finish the question)." The teacher in the example has provided seed questions that keep the students focused on content and allow the teacher to determine the general level of student understanding.

Power Zone

The final structural component of FSGPT is provided when the teacher remains in the power zone throughout the student conversations. While in the power zone, the teacher is in the best position to ensure that the students remain focused on the task at hand, participating in an academic discussion. Also, critical insights, examples, and connections that are made by individual students can be shared with the entire class. In addition, any points of misunderstanding made by individual students or shared by the collective class can be addressed either immediately or during the next section of teacher talk.

Adult Language/Student Language

As longtime practitioners, the authors are convinced that numerous bilingual students populate every classroom in

America—not bilingual in terms of national languages (although that does exist), but bilingual in terms of the ability to speak and comprehend both adult language and student language. This issue as it relates to instruction is that, as a teacher, one's primary form of feedback on the quality of the lesson is provided by the students who can most easily converse with an adult. Due to their ability to converse with every person in the class, these students are engaged, inquisitive, and often insightful. Unfortunately, the feedback that these students provide the teacher often hides the fact that the other students, those who do not speak "adult," are essentially swimming upstream and that the longer the teacher talks, the further behind these students fall. Fortunately, the fundamental practice of frequent, small-group, purposeful talk about the learning provides a remedy to this common classroom malady.

Time to Translate

One should recognize that in general, a student who understands "adult speak" has an advantage in understanding the lesson over the student who only understands "student speak." By providing students with the opportunity to discuss with each other the topic at hand every ten to fifteen minutes, the students who understand both adult speak and student speak have the opportunity to translate for the students who only speak student. From an anecdotal perspective, this simple process has a dramatic effect on the climate and culture of a classroom. Students quickly take ownership of the learning, and, with an overall student focus shifting to academic inquiry as opposed to tracking time and staving off boredom, learning improves. As teachers become more adept in selecting seed questions and students more adept at their communication skills, numerous embedded benefits to the quality of instruction will quickly become apparent.

Student Retention

First and foremost, the fundamental practice of FSGPT makes a significant positive impact on retention. There are a number of reasons for this, but the discussion will begin with the most obvious. During the course of instruction, teachers with even minimal experience quickly begin to sense that there are some students in the classroom who truly are beginning to understand the concept that is being taught. At that point, it would behoove the teacher to have a process, practice, or strategy that would cement that learning in place and make it permanent. One way for a teacher to do this would be to create an opportunity for the students to teach the skill or concept to someone else. A small-group, purposeful talk session provides this opportunity.

Additionally, during the course of instruction, a teacher will realize that along with the students who "get it," there are some students who are struggling to understand the concept being taught. At this point, the teacher is faced with a decision. The teacher can continue to push ahead at full speed, leaving student understanding in his or her wake. This, unfortunately, is an all-too-common practice that the authors do not recommend. The teacher could stop and deliver the instruction again, often more slowly, more loudly, and with increased frustration. Again, though a common practice, this is not a recommended action. The teacher could also stop and provide the opportunity for a brief peer-to-peer tutoring session. This is the teacher response that the authors recommend. FSGPT provides opportunities for students who get "it" to get "it" better and for students who do not get "it" to hear the material again, but this time in a language (student talk) that they better understand. This reinforces the intent of the lesson for some of the class and immediately reteaches the material for those in the class who missed the intent of the lesson the first time it was presented.

The Primacy/Recency Effect

FSGPT allows teachers to better harness the power of the primacy/recency effect. Early research on this effect dates back to the 1880s, when Hermann Ebbinghaus published his work on the processes of learning and forgetting. The primacy/recency effect, simply stated, points out that "…in a learning episode, we tend to remember best that which comes first, and remember second best that which comes last. We tend to remember least that which comes just past the middle of the episode" (Sousa 2001, 88).

Most teachers, in the course of instruction, have just one start and one finish in their lesson cycle: the beginning of the class and the end of the class. This is yet another reason why a quality lesson frame is such a powerful instructional tool. When the brain is most alert, the lesson frame highlights what is most important about the lesson, the critical instructional concept (primacy), and the student's final demonstration of that concept (recency).

Fortunately, the brain does not track time just in terms of class periods; it also tracks time in terms of state changes. A state change is simply a change in physical or mental state.

By introducing multiple state changes during the course of a class period, the teacher is able to create multiple starts and finishes, thus facilitating the possible creation of not just vibrant memories at the actual beginning and ending of class, but multiple vibrant memories throughout the class. The charts below illustrate this process.

Traditional Fifty-Five-Minute Class Period

Activity	Relative Time	Type of Memory
Start of Class	Primacy	Vibrant
Instruction	Middle	Less Vibrant Over Time
End of Class	Recency	Vibrant

Fifty-Five-Minute Class Period with a Single Small Group Purposeful Talk Session Included

Activity	Relative Time	Type of Memory
Start of Class	Primacy	Vibrant
Instruction	Middle	Less Vibrant Over Time
Stop Instruction	Recency	Vibrant
Start Discussion	Primacy	Vibrant
Stop Discussion	Recency	Vibrant
Start Instruction	Primacy	Vibrant
Instruction	Middle	Less Vibrant Over Time
End of Class	Recency	Vibrant

As the charts above so clearly illustrate, in a traditional classroom, students are left with two vibrant memories at the end of the class period. If, during that same class, the teacher introduces just one session of small-group, purposeful talk, at the end of the class period, students could have access to as many as six vibrant memories relating to the content. Based on their experience and ongoing observations, the authors firmly believe that regardless of a student's innate cognitive ability, the more content he or she remembers, the better he or she will perform academically.

Attention Span

As previously discussed, the use of FSGPT introduces state changes during the course of instruction. In addition to leveraging the primacy/recency effect, these state changes also provide the teacher with an effective vehicle for managing student attention spans. Consider the typical adult; under normal circumstances, this person will have an attention span of ten to fifteen minutes. "For teens the figure is eight to ten minutes…and for students 12 years and under the figures become even more drastically reduced" (Allen 2009, 31). But as is the case with the primacy/recency effect, a state change can reset the attention span clock. By introducing a small-group purposeful talk session, the teacher can circumvent the loss of student attention and the ensuing wave of boredom that follows.

Consider the typical classroom. As is the case with most teachers, this teacher begins class teaching at full speed, understanding that he or she must cover a certain amount of material in a set period of time. For the first ten to fifteen minutes of class time, the class operates well and students are attentive. During the next ten to fifteen minutes of the class, students begin to get a little restless. The teacher most likely responds with some individual student corrections, an attempt to pick up the pace of the instructional task, or both. Finally, during the next ten to fifteen minutes of class, students will often begin to get unruly, leaving the teacher to resort to either the big bribe or the big threat. The big bribe is "If you just behave, I will give you... (some type of bribe)." The big threat is "If you do not behave, you will all go to the office" (or some such equally onerous outcome). At the point of the big bribe or the big threat, the class has been crushed by a wave of boredom.

The strategic use of FSGPT allows the teacher to reset student attention spans and surf the boredom wave. When a teacher tells the class, "Let's stop what we are doing; turn to your partner and discuss..." the teacher has created a state change. This state change resets the attention span allowing students to continue to successfully focus on the learning outcome. Now the teacher has created a classroom instructional cycle that looks similar to the following:

Ten to fifteen minutes of engaged instruction; followed by,

One to three minutes of engaged conversation; followed by another,

Ten to fifteen minutes of engaged instruction; followed by another,

One to three minutes of engaged conversation, and so on.

This teacher is able to purposefully manage the amount of effective instructional minutes and maintain high levels of student engagement.

Instructional Rigor and Relevance

Up to this point, the arguments for FSGPT have centered on its effect on student retention of the content. But one should also consider the effect FSGPT has on the level of instructional rigor and relevance. In the current education environment, teachers are constantly reminded of the importance of increasing both the rigor and relevance of instruction. The concept of rigor, or the level of cognition, as described by Dr. Benjamin Bloom in his now famous taxonomy, is almost universally recognized by teachers. In 2000, Anderson et al. published a revised cognitive taxonomy. Bloom's original taxonomy, the amended taxonomy, and descriptors of student tasks that correlate to the levels of cognition are presented in the chart below.

Lead Your School Rigor Groupings	Original Bloom Categories	New Bloom Categories	Description of Student Work
Low Rigor	Knowledge	Remembering	• Define • Find • List • Match • Select
Low Rigor	Comprehension	Understanding	• Calculate • Describe • Locate • Outline • Review
Mid Rigor	Application	Applying	• Apply • Build • Model • Plan • Utilize
Mid Rigor	Analysis	Analyzing	• Analyze • Compare • Diagram • Edit • Transform
High Rigor	Synthesis	Evaluating	• Compose • Create • Improve • Revise • Summarize
High Rigor	Evaluation	Creating	• Appraise • Debate • Judge • Support • Verify

The concept of relevance, which is gaining prominence in the discussions on instruction, represents the attempt to have the student connect to the content on a personal level. The consensus of curriculum experts is that currently, both the rigor and relevance of typical classroom instruction is lacking. Based on personal observations and the analysis of the data from tens of thousands of classroom observations (Cain and Laird, unpublished research, 2010), the authors cannot refute this. To help teachers increase the rigor and relevance of their lessons, many curriculum experts offer a solution similar to the following:

> *"Teachers, we are going to pull you from the classroom for some extended training on instructional rigor and/or relevance. Then we expect you to spend significant time developing and planning lessons that reflect this training. Finally, we expect you to teach these new rigorous and relevant lessons in addition to the lessons you are already expected to teach."*

Is it any wonder why teachers leave the profession? The authors' foray into this fray is limited to the following two beliefs. First, the issues relating to the rigor and relevance of classroom instruction are driven as much, if not more, by curricular content than teacher decisions. Most curricula are written in the content area (naturally) and are presented at the knowledge and comprehension level. Classroom instruction reflects this. Second, improving the delivery of instruction rather than improving the quality of the content better serves the teacher. FSGPT provides the means to do just that, allowing any teacher to quickly and easily increase the rigor and relevance of any lesson.

How this works is surprisingly straightforward. First, consider instructional relevance. Given the three basic categories of relevance discussed earlier (in-content, across-content, and real-world), when students engage in discussions about the content, they bring in familiar examples which they use in conversation to describe and explain the learning topic. Those examples come from all three relevance areas, but primarily, they seem to come from outside the content area. Thus, instead of the teacher spending precious time trying to emphasize the relevance of the content to the students (which, in many cases, actually seems to decrease relevance for the student), the teacher simply provides students with the opportunity to create their own relevance. This is a solution the authors wholeheartedly recommend that every teacher work to implement.

Second, consider instructional rigor. It does not matter at what level of rigor overall instruction is delivered. Through the use of the seed question provided to the small groups, the teacher can increase the level of rigor at will. Again, consider a simple geometry lesson; a lesson where the teacher is simply introducing the shape of a triangle and the shape of a square. The overall lesson might focus on the recognition of the two shapes. Mastery of this lesson would entail the students operating at the knowledge and comprehension levels of cognition. However, in the course of the lesson, through the use of FSGPT, the teacher could ask a question such as:

"How are triangles and squares similar?"

In the one to three minutes that students spend answering this question, the level of instructional rigor increases from comprehension to analysis, as represented on Bloom's taxonomy.

As further proof of how this practice can be used with any lesson, the content that has been presented in this book can be used as an example. If a trainer was using this book as an instructional resource, at this point, the trainer could introduce the following short discussion activity:

> *"Teachers, we have now discussed three of the five fundamental practices of effective instruction: Frame the Lesson; Work in the Power Zone; and Frequent, Small-Group, Purposeful Talk about the Learning. Now, with your discussion buddy, quietly discuss how you would implement these three practices in your classroom. You will have three minutes to discuss this, and then we will share our thoughts with the entire group."*

The discussion of a list of practices generally falls within the knowledge and comprehension levels of Bloom's taxonomy. But the use of this question moves the rigor to (at least) the application level. As an added bonus, because the seed question forced the learner to consider how he or she would personally use these practices in another setting (his or her own classroom), the relevance of the lesson shifted to the real-world level. Thus, a simple three-minute discussion after the introduction of three simple practices took a low-rigor/low-relevance lesson and shifted it to the level of mid-rigor/high-relevance. The authors hope, based on these two examples, the reader will recognize that it is a much more efficient use of teacher time to develop a handful of academically rigorous question stems (see chart, "Talk Like a Genius Question Stems" below) to use during a lesson as opposed to spending time creating an entire bank of new, more rigorous and relevant lessons.

Putting It All Together

For a practice that seems simple on paper, effective FSGPT implementation requires deliberate planning, execution, and reflection on the part of the teacher. Consider first the act of allowing students to talk, *purposefully* and *academically*. In the initial attempts, this effort will often be messy. A student-to-student conversation is almost always social in nature. In addition, many students are not used to talking to each other academically, having rarely been given the opportunity. This academic type of conversation will be awkward for them at first, but given multiple supervised and guided opportunities, they will rapidly improve.

Additionally, the development of effective seed questions requires some planning on the part of the teacher. Without advance preparation, the questions that teachers develop on the fly are either closed questions (a question that can be answered with a single word or a short phrase) or low rigor (knowledge or comprehension), or both. This is not because teachers are unable to develop more academically rigorous questions; it is because under conditions of stress, the brain defaults to the lowest common denominator (i.e., low-rigor questions with simple, obvious answers). The attempt on the part of the teacher to instruct a class, manage a class, and provide meaningful questions certainly qualifies as a stressful condition. A successful way to counter this stress is with the use of a "question stem wall." A question stem wall is simply a bulletin board or other designated space that has open-ended question stems posted. The purpose of an open-ended question is to provoke thought, reflection, or have the learner make connections. On the question stem wall, these open-ended questions are categorized by the level of thinking required to answer them (rigor level), and they are visible and available to all.

Talk Like a Genius Question Stems

Smart Questions (Knowledge & Comprehension)	Smarter Questions (Application & Analysis)	Smartest Questions (Synthesis & Evaluation)
Who is it that...?	How would you use...?	What would happen if...?
Tell why...?	How is this similar to...?	Develop a plan to...?
Give an example of...?	Contrast this to...?	Find a better solution to...?
What do you think will happen next...?	What is the relationship between...?	What is the most important...?

When first introduced to FSGPT, many teachers want to implement the practice immediately. They start with the best of intentions, begin to teach, and by the time they remember to stop and let the students talk, numerous opportunities have passed. This is simply because the teacher has yet to develop a "stop-and-talk" rhythm. An easy way to quickly create this rhythm is to purchase an inexpensive kitchen timer (egg timer). At the beginning of class, set the timer for ten minutes. When the timer goes off, the teacher simply completes his or her thought and then the students discuss the introduced concepts using a preplanned seed question. Once the students complete their discussions, the teacher resets the timer for another ten minutes and repeats the cycle.

There is a twist to the egg timer strategy that many teachers find effective. The authors have named this the "busy teacher timer strategy," and it works in the following manner. The busy teacher realizes that it will be difficult to manage the classroom, teach the content, and now track time in ten-to-fifteen-minute increments. So the busy teacher does not even attempt to try this. Rather, the busy teacher walks into the classroom with the timer in hand, locates his or her most behaviorally challenged student, presents the timer to that student, and says something along the lines of, "I have a very important job for you. I want you to help me teach the class. Do you want to try?"

The busy teacher then quickly teaches the student how to use the timer. Now the teacher remains focused on managing the class, teaching the content, and stopping when the timer goes off. The student takes care of the rest.

Frequent, small-group, purposeful talk about the learning is a powerful instructional tool. Its effective use has a tremendous impact on student behavior, student retention, and the depth and quality of the presented content. In fact, based on the use of this practice in numerous settings with learners of all age levels and all ability levels, the authors are willing to make this promise to teachers:

> *"You can teach what you have always taught. You can teach it almost the same way you have always taught it. Just add frequent, small-group, purposeful talk. More of your students will learn more of what you want them to know."*

CHAPTER SIX

Recognize and Reinforce

As addressed in chapter 2, "Overview," recognition and reinforcement address two sides of the learning coin. One side of the coin is related to academic issues, and the other side is related to social and behavioral issues. This chapter will address first the academic side of the coin and then the social and behavioral side of the coin.

Academic Recognition

Recognition from an academic standpoint is the recognition of academic success, and academic success must be a really big deal. As educators, we readily give recognition to students who reach the pinnacles of academic success; the students who earned an A on a test, an A in the class, honor roll status, a high class rank, or meet the requirements of graduation all receive various forms and levels of recognition from adults. However, as educators, we generally miss the opportunity to recognize the interim levels of academic success that represent progress toward achieving higher academic goals. For example, take four random students from a typical class. Justin has not turned in a single homework assignment for the past three weeks, but today, he did remember to bring his homework to class and turn it in. This is a big deal for Justin. Johnny has never scored higher than seventy-four on a test. Today, he scored an eighty-three. This is a big deal for Johnny. Brittany made the honor roll for the first time. This is a big deal for Brittany. Finally, Kandace scored at the commended performance level on the state accountability exam. This is a big deal for Kandace. These are four examples of academic success in this classroom, yet in most cases, as a teacher, one would recognize the success of Brittany and Kandace while overlooking the opportunity to recognize the smaller, but perhaps more important, interim successes of Justin and Johnny.

Academic Reinforcement

From the academic standpoint, reinforcement is the reinforcement of the work and/or effort that is required to achieve a certain level of academic success. As is the case with academic recognition, academic reinforcement is a really big deal. Yet the reinforcement of work and effort seems to represent a significant blind spot for many teachers. From the authors' perspective, there is a logical explanation for this observation. Many, if not most, teachers entered the field of education because they enjoyed school. They were successful in school, and they were intrinsically motivated to complete the tasks that were assigned to them in class. As such, they did not have to think about the work it took to succeed academically, because in most cases, it did not seem like work at all. For example, when they were students, both authors were avid readers. The requirement to go home and read a chapter was not seen as work. In many cases, it was actually review, because they had previously read the chapter for enjoyment. Thus, the teacher who rarely, or never, viewed school tasks as work has a difficult time reinforcing the distinct tasks that must be accomplished by the non-school-oriented student to successfully fulfill the expectations of the class.

Once again, let's consider the example of Justin and his homework. For Justin to have turned in his homework today, he had to have completed a number of steps. First, he had to write down the homework assignment on the previous day. Second, once at home, he had to remember that he had homework. Third, he actually had to do the homework assignment. Fourth, he had to remember to bring the homework assignment back to school. Fifth, he had to remember to bring the homework assignment back to class. Sixth, and finally, he had to turn in the homework assignment. How is Justin not exhausted? This represents a significant amount of work on Justin's part, since, based on the evidence (the lack of turned-in homework assignments), the process of completing and turning in homework is an activity that Justin does not intuitively navigate. This work must be outlined and reinforced if turning in homework is to become a regular occurrence for Justin, and it is the observant and insightful teacher who will notice this situation and act based on this understanding.

Benefits of Academic Reinforcement and Recognition

The benefits of academic reinforcement and recognition are many. And, unlike a host of instructional recommendations, the effect of the practice has been quantified in numerous research studies. Although these studies draw differing conclusions on the practice, Marzano et al., in *Classroom Instruction that Works* (2001), report that according to the reviewed research, the use of effective reinforcement produced between a 20 to 48 percentile gain in student achievement (51). Teachers must recognize that a 20 to 48 percentile improvement in student performance is potentially life changing. From a system standpoint, a school can move from a "watch list" to academic stability. From the standpoint of the teacher, a career in jeopardy can transition to a career of recognized success. But both of these pale in light of what it can mean to a student. An improvement in achievement of this magnitude can represent the difference between failing or passing a course, graduating or not graduating, attending the college of one's choice or not pursuing additional education, etc.

Recognition of academic success at any level provides students with the motivation to continue in their pursuit of academic success. Reinforcement of the work and effort it takes to achieve academic success builds habits and understandings that students can access throughout their academic career and well into their adult life. In the authors' experience, many students, especially those labeled "at-risk," often see little connection between their effort and earned reward. They view life as a series of random actions over which they have little, if any, control. The more at risk the students the more important the recognition of work and effort become. If one was to ask a group of at-risk students why one student is more successful than another, one would often hear responses such as, "She is smart," or "He is lucky," or "The teacher likes her," or "She likes school," and so on. The connection between the academic work and academic success is essentially invisible to these students. However, when the teacher addresses the fact that when students complete discrete tasks, the sum of those tasks will equal a level of success, and when the teacher then reinforces students as they complete those tasks, students quickly begin to understand that their efforts have a direct impact on the reward (success) they reap. At this point, the student is no longer the victim of fate (lucky or unlucky); the student controls his or her actions (work or do not work). This is a critical juncture because now the student is building an understanding that individual effort and hard work (work ethic) are of value. "Reinforcing effort can help teach students one of the most valuable lessons they can learn—the harder you try, the more successful you are" (Marzano 2001, 59).

Social and Behavioral Recognition

Recognition from the social and behavioral perspective addresses the concepts (or principles) of personalization and specificity. In layman's terms, personalization is simply providing clarity in relation to who is being addressed. Instead of applying comments to broad groups of students, the teacher addresses specific groups of students or, better yet, individual students. Specificity addresses the need to clearly state the behavior or action that warranted the attention. To better illustrate this, consider three students walking down a hallway. While walking as a group, one student, almost unconsciously, bends over to pick up a piece of paper on the floor and then correctly disposes of that piece of paper in a wastebasket as the students continue on their way to the next class. If a teacher is witness to this act and says nothing to the student, that teacher has missed an excellent opportunity to recognize a positive and socially responsible student behavior.

If a teacher is witness to this act and simply says, "Good job," this is better than saying nothing, but the teacher has missed the opportunity to recognize the specific student (personalization) and the specific positive behavior (specificity) that the teacher observed. The effect of the teacher's general comment is diffused and misguided, as opposed to being focused and on target. Essentially, the student who picked up and threw away the piece of paper receives a vague positive acknowledgement for the positive behavior. Unfortunately, the two students who ignored the piece of paper on the floor receive the same vague positive acknowledgment for their negative behavior (not picking up the trash). The question then becomes: which student and what behavior was the teacher actually recognizing? For this general comment to be an example of effective recognition requires the students to know exactly what the teacher's comment is referring to and to who it is addressed. In the authors' experience, this level of student understanding is less common than most teachers realize.

If, however, a teacher who is witness to the act of one student in a group picking up and throwing away a piece of paper says, "Thank you, Shelton, for picking that up. I appreciate your effort to keep our school clean."

The teacher has demonstrated the use of personalized and specific recognition. Shelton and the other two students know that Shelton is the recipient of the teacher's attention. The three students also know exactly why Shelton has received the recognition. He picked up and threw away the piece of paper, while the other two did not. Interestingly, Shelton now feels better about his action, the other two students are aware of what precipitated the recognition, and all three students are more likely to repeat the behavior in the future—all because the teacher recognized and seized the opportunity to provide personal and specific recognition to the advantage of the students, and, in the case of this example, even the school.

These same principles of personalization and specificity apply to the recognition of academic behaviors as well. For example, which of these following two recognition comments by a teacher would be considered most effective?

"Good job, class. Most of you turned in your homework this week."

Or,

"Good job, table group three. Your table has turned in 100 percent of your homework this week."

The second statement is considered superior because it addresses personalization (table group three) and specificity

(100 percent of homework assignments turned in), whereas the first comment is not as focused and is therefore less effective.

Social and Behavioral Reinforcement

Reinforcement as used here follows the operant conditioning theory of B. F. Skinner. The basic idea of operant conditioning is that the consequences of a certain behavior strongly influence the chances of the behavior increasing or decreasing. It is not the authors' intention to delve further into the specifics of Skinner's theory. However, additional text, such as *Psychology Applied to Teaching*, by Snowman and Biehler (2006, 212–231) or others will assist the reader interested in a more thorough examination of the topic.

For the purpose of understanding social and behavioral reinforcement within the context of the classroom, it is the reinforcement of the behaviors that the teacher wants to see more of, and the removal of reinforcement for behaviors that the teacher wants to see less of. Unfortunately, in far too many cases, teachers actually do the reverse. An excellent example of this is how many teachers respond to the student who is late to class. The behavior the teacher wants to see more of is students arriving for class on time and prepared to start their lessons. The best way to reinforce this behavior is for the teacher to warmly greet students at the classroom door, welcome them to the class with an "I'm glad to see you today," and remind them to get ready because instruction will commence as soon as the bell rings. Then, when the bell rings, the teacher should have the students immediately begin an instructional task that has meaning. Every student who has arrived on time has had his or her on-time behavior reinforced by the teacher (standing by the door) in a positive and personal manner. However, all too many teachers are not at the door when students arrive and make little attempt to acknowledge their arrival to the classroom. Thus, the behavior that the teacher wants to see more of (students on time to class) receives inconsistent, if any, attention. But once the tardy bell rings, the student who is late to class receives a lot of attention, in the form of a teacher reprimand, a tardy demerit of some sort, a trip to the office, or some combination of the three. The behavior the teacher does not want to see (students late to class) is now the behavior that is receiving significant attention.

By reinforcing the behaviors the teacher wants to see (through increased attention and/or extrinsic reward), the teacher is able to shape student behavior and teach students the behaviors that they need to engage in to be successful in the classroom. Though this may seem to take longer to achieve the desired behavioral results than the use of negative consequences, in the long run, the results are much longer lasting. It has been the experience of the authors, as both teachers and school leaders, that negative consequences will change student behaviors while, and as long as, the student knows that adults are watching. However, positive reinforcement will change student behavior when adults are watching and, more importantly, even when the student knows that adults are not watching.

Putting It All Together

When the authors conduct Fundamental Five presentations and trainings across the country, they poll their audiences on which practice the audience members believe is the most important. In nearly every case, recognition and reinforcement receives the most votes. Yet for a number of teachers, this is the most difficult of the Fundamental Five practices to implement. In the authors' opinion, there are two primary reasons behind this difficulty. First, the successful implementation of this practice runs contrary to the attitudes and personality of many adults. Even the authors readily admit that this practice did not come naturally to them. However, if the teacher remains in the power zone and actively looks for opportunities to recognize and reinforce students (and does so), the positive change in student performance, behaviors, and attitudes will create an incentive to continue the practice. The increased teacher use of recognition and reinforcement in turn builds increased teacher skill and comfort in the use of the practice. This is a case where one is encouraged to "fake it until you make it."

The second reason why many teachers find this practice difficult to implement is that managing a classroom is a stressful endeavor. When one operates under stress, it is easy for one to default to one's baseline behaviors or habits. Changing one's habits takes conscious effort, time, and support. Add the stress of changing what one looks for and responds to in an already stressful situation and the transition can easily become overwhelming to some.

To increase the pace of implementation of this practice in the classroom, many teachers report that the following strategies prove to be helpful. First, teachers are advised to create a list of two to five targeted student behaviors or accomplishments that they want to encourage. When the teacher observes these behaviors or accomplishments, he or she should recognize and reinforce the student in question, remembering the principles of personalization and specificity. When the frequency and quality of the target behaviors or accomplishments are at a level of teacher satisfaction, revise the list and add some new targeted behaviors. Second, along with recognizing students who have earned high grades in the classroom, the teacher is encouraged to recognize student effort and improvement. Just as an A is worthy of celebration, so is a fifteen-point improvement in a student's achievement results. Finally, teachers are encouraged to rely on and support their peers. The willingness to ask for and/or offer assistance changes the dynamic of the professional learning community from one where many pretend to be perfect to one that recognizes that improvement in instructional craft requires collaboration and support.

Teachers who deliberately engage in the practice of recognition and reinforcement quickly create classroom environments that are nurturing, engaging, and empowering to an increased number of students. These classrooms begin to drive increased student performance because student work and effort are validated and rewarded. Finally, as documented in the book *Classroom Instruction that Works* (Marzano 2001, 49–59), a teacher can teach what he or she has always taught, in the manner he or she has always taught it, and simply by adding effective, meaningful, and significant recognition and reinforcement, individual student achievement and overall classroom performance can increase significantly. One teacher, when realizing the enormity of this gain, stated eloquently: "I may have been born at night, but I wasn't born last night. I would be crazy not to get better at this."

For Your Consideration

There are some adults who believe that the use of extrinsic rewards actually reduces the student's desire to work for the love of learning. For those adults, the authors point out that research consistently shows that the purposeful use of extrinsic rewards to change behaviors leads to the behavior being used by the learner to satisfy intrinsic motivations.

Other adults believe that engaging in a task for an extrinsic reward either cheapens the task or represents some form of bribery. For those adults, the authors simply ask, "Do you love your job? If so, do you do it for free?"

Great teachers realize that students are motivated to work for a variety of reasons and work to identify and provide those motivators.

CHAPTER SEVEN

Write Critically

Critical writing, defined as writing for the purpose of organizing, clarifying, defending, refuting, analyzing, dissecting, connecting, and/or expanding on ideas or concepts, is currently the least frequently used of the five practices that the authors have identified to be fundamental to effective instruction. In his book *Results Now* (2006), Mike Schmoker documents that based on a study of 1,500 classroom observations, the number of classrooms in which students were either writing or using rubrics was 0 percent (18). For those who doubt the validity of this observation, the authors sympathize, as they also were initially skeptical. But their own analysis of the data from hundreds of initial classroom observations has yielded similar results. The bottom line is that when it comes to writing critically in the classroom, teachers do not have students do enough of it.

Based in part on discussions with educators from all grade levels and all content areas and their own experiences in the classroom, it is the authors' opinion that this lack of critical writing is primarily due to teachers' misconceptions of what constitutes critical writing. Many teachers seem to operate under the misconception that critical writing is a function of weight. By "weight," it is meant that the teachers believe that a critical writing exercise requires numerous pages, numerous footnotes, and numerous revisions. Alternatively, some teachers seem to believe that a critical writing assignment must take a significant amount of time and must culminate in a perfectly spelled, typed, and ready-for-publication student product. Other teachers believe that critical writing is the responsibility of the English/language arts and writing teachers or that writing critically does not fit into their content area. Though the reader may feel as if there is some overgeneralization in the preceding descriptions, the authors ask for some leeway in order to illustrate their point. Given the way that most teachers seem to view critical writing, is it any wonder why it is observed infrequently in classrooms? By focusing on the end product, teachers misunderstand the power of the process of writing critically.

"Everything we write is a potential learning experience. Writing is a systematic process for learning essential meanings" (Paul and Elder 2007, 8). The process of writing critically requires the learner to take a subconscious idea, expand on that idea, connect it to other subconscious ideas, and bring that to the conscious level through the tangible act of writing.

To gain knowledge, we must construct it in our minds. Writing what we are trying to internalize helps us achieve that purpose. When we are able to make connections in writing, we begin to take ownership of these connections. To do this we must learn how to identify core ideas...and then explain those ideas in writing... (Paul and Elder 2007, 8).

When one views "critical writing" as a process, as opposed to an end product, then the time spent, weight, and perfection are no longer critical variables. Putting focused thought on paper is the important element. Through this lens, critical writing can take on many forms. A critical writing exercise can consist of a simple list, a short comparison paragraph, a quick summary, a mind map, purposeful note taking, a written exit ticket, or even a formal essay or term paper. It must be noted that critical writing is not copying, a popular instructional activity that essentially transforms entire classrooms into slow-speed Xerox machines. Neither is critical writing a "fill in the blank" activity or "free" writing. Without debating the merits of these activities, the reader is reminded to focus on the key term *critical*, which indicates the intent to distill abstract thoughts into concrete understandings.

The Raw Power of Critical Writing

The authors cannot overemphasize the power of critical writing. Consider three instructional practices addressed in the book *Classroom Instruction that Works* (Marzano 2001): identifying similarities and differences, summarization, and note taking. These three practices represent the pinnacle of effective instruction identified in the book, and all three can be accomplished through a well-designed critical writing exercise. Given the research, the critical writing activity of identifying similarities and differences can increase student performance from 31 to 46 percentile points. For summarization, student performance gains can range between 23 and 47 percentile points, and note taking can produce a corresponding student performance gain of between 13 and 44 percentile points. With the current focus on school accountability, the incentive to increase the amount of critical writing in the classroom in order to realize those gains in student achievement should not be in question. Clearly, critical writing is essential for academic improvement. However, raw numbers and campus accountability scores do not tell the whole story. Writing critically has a dramatic impact on the individual student.

> *Students, who think critically use writing as an important tool both for communicating important ideas and for learning... to deepen their understanding of important concepts and to clarify interrelationships between concepts...they use writing as an important tool for learning ideas deeply and permanently (Paul and Elder 2006, 5).*

The act of writing critically encapsulates the learning. It forces the learner to refine and distill a concept or idea to its critical message and in many cases connect that critical message to other critical messages. It allows the learner to improve retention through "...the process whereby long-term memory preserves a learning in such a way that it can locate, identify, and retrieve it accurately in the future" (Sousa 2001, 85).

Writing critically increases both the amount of material that can be recalled by the learner and the speed at which it can be recalled. When a student can remember more content and process that content more efficiently, the student has a greater likelihood of enjoying success in the classroom.

In terms of direct benefit to the student, writing critically on a regular basis increases overall literacy skills. The process of reading and writing are so entwined that, from a cognitive standpoint, they are essentially the same skill. "There is an intimate relationship between reading and writing well. Any significant deficiency in reading entails a parallel deficiency in writing. Any significant deficiency in writing entails a parallel deficiency in reading" (Paul and Elder 2006, 2).

This is valuable instructional information, because the research indicates that the key to increasing literacy skills is to increase the amount of time spent on literacy activities, and that would mean "…converting current amounts of time and hard work from unproductive 'stuff' to literacy activities that would be far more meaningful to both students and teachers" (Schmoker 2006, 98). This helps to explain the emphasis and, in many cases, directives from district and campus leadership for teachers to embed reading and critical writing in all content areas. However, given both curricular pacing constraints and teacher skill sets, directing someone to include these activities in the classroom and having it actually occur are two different things. Where reading represents a significant investment in classroom time and requires an enhanced instructional skill set to support students who have difficulty reading, writing is easier for teachers to support and modify to fit the activities scheduled in the class. Based on a better understanding of the components of literacy (reading and writing), when students write about what they have learned in a given class and do this in all classes, each student has had the time devoted to improving his or her literacy skills significantly increased. As students increase their literacy ability, the options available to them, both short term and long term, are also increased and improved. While this is beneficial for high-achieving students, it has the potential to be life changing for low-achieving students. When one considers that the reading requirements[2] for many entry-level blue-collar jobs are similar to the reading requirements for the freshman year of college (see chart below), to not embed literacy opportunities in every class represents a significant disservice to all students.

Grade Range or Post-Secondary Category	Recommended Lexile Range
Second and Third Grade	450–790
Fourth and Fifth Grade	770–980
Sixth through Eighth Grade	955–1155
Ninth and Tenth Grade	1080–1305
Eleventh and Career/College Ready	1215–1355
Citizenship	1100–1205
Workplace	1010–1280
Community College	1100–1290
University	1200–1400
Professional Career	1350+

Source material for chart from, www.Lexile.com

---

2   Reading requirements for the purpose of this book are measured though the use of Lexile scores. A Lexile score is a quantitative measure of reading level/reading ability. For additional information, visit www.Lexile.com.

A Confession

Both authors were classroom teachers (Cain taught math and Laird taught social studies) when the early emphasis on reading and writing across the content areas came into vogue. Both received the directive to increase the amount of reading and writing in their classrooms and both continued to teach as they had always taught. The reason, no one told them or showed them how this was to be accomplished, and it was not part of their evaluation.

When both authors were principals, they repeated the cycle, directing teachers to increase the amount of reading and writing in every class, yet still providing no meaningful classroom support or effective teacher training. They did, however, wring their hands when they observed no change in classroom practices (as their principals had done years before).

The sharing of their current understanding that writing and reading are inseparable and providing ways to embed more literacy in the classroom is their way to support current teachers and administrators to close the knowing/doing gap that existed in their classrooms and on their campuses.

Rigor and Relevance

After years of experience teaching in the classroom, leading schools, and leading school systems, coupled with literally thousands of classroom observations representing all grade levels and content areas, the authors are of the firm opinion that most attempts by teachers to add instructional rigor in the classroom are, first and foremost, much less frequent than most educators believe and, second, are contrived, poorly executed, and/or overly orchestrated. The reader should understand that this is not meant as an indictment. In fact, it is a testament to the difficulty of the task. Fortunately, there is a simple solution, and critical writing provides it. A critical writing activity allows the teacher to stretch the rigor of any lesson, maintain the higher level of rigor for an extended period of time, and do so in a natural and authentic fashion.

Consider the following critical writing exercise. If one was teaching a class about the Fundamental Five, at this point in the discussion, the teacher could ask the students to quickly create a list of the Fundamental Five practices of effective instruction (Frame the Lesson; Work in the Power Zone; Frequent, Small-Group, Purposeful Talk about the Learning; Recognize and Reinforce; Write Critically). This would represent rigor at the knowledge level of Bloom's taxonomy. From that list, the teacher could then have the students indicate which of the Fundamental Five practices they deem to be the most important. This would represent rigor at the analysis level of Bloom's taxonomy. The teacher could then have the students defend their selection of the most important Fundamental Five practice. This represents rigor at the evaluation level of Bloom's taxonomy. Finally, the teacher could have the students read and discuss their arguments in small groups (FSGPT), extending the length of time that students are operating at higher levels of cognition. This type of critical writing activity, which is appropriate in almost any instructional setting, quickly drives classroom rigor to the evaluation level of Bloom's taxonomy and keeps it there for a period of time. The beauty of this particular activity is that it can be completed in as little as ten minutes. Though ten minutes of instructional time is a precious commodity, if writing critically (at the higher levels of Bloom's taxonomy) replaces an instructional activity of lower rigor, the trade-off would seemingly benefit both the student and the teacher.

The introduction of critical writing activities in the classroom also provides the opportunity to increase the level of relevance for students. The reader will recall from the discussion in chapter 3, "Framing the Lesson," that relevance is increased when the concept or skill being taught is connected to other parts of the student's world. When students write critically, they often connect the concept being addressed to other concepts that they are familiar with from both academic and nonacademic settings. This occurs even with writing prompts that are related directly to the content area. With the selection of a correct writing prompt, the teacher can specifically manage student-developed relevance, as opposed to relying on teacher-driven relevance. An example of teacher-driven relevance is when the teacher attempts to increase the relevance of a lesson by pointing out to the class, "This is how you could use this skill in the real world." Relevance presented this way is the equivalent of an interesting factoid, such as, "baking soda can also be used as a toothpaste substitute." This may be an interesting fact, but it is one that will be promptly forgotten by all but the most trivia-inclined student.

On the other hand, the teacher who presents a concept and then instructs students to "write down what other uses for baking soda of which you are aware" positions the student to connect, on his or her own, the presented concept to other areas of his or her world. This is important, because when the student makes the extended relevance connection in a way that makes sense to him or her, the use of the knowledge has extended beyond the status of mere factoid. Through the act of critical writing, the teacher has increased the probability that the content is owned by the student.

Formative Assessment

Critical writing provides the student and the teacher with an excellent source of formative assessment material. Information is formative when the teacher and student adjust their actions based on what the information reveals. During the critical writing activity, the student is able to identify gaps in his or her learning, questions he or she wants to ask, and/or insights he or she has developed. This positions the student to engage with the teacher and the class in ways that better meet his or her interests and needs. By reviewing the critical writing sample, the teacher can quickly assess the level of student understanding and quickly establish if the student is making appropriate and meaningful connections between new content and prior content. Based on that assessment, the teacher makes purposeful adjustments to his or her instruction, for example, speeding up, slowing down, reviewing, regrouping, and/or providing individual support.

The critical writing activity is always assessed. But it does not have to be formally assessed each and every time. Simply put, this means that a grade does not have to be entered every time the student puts pen to paper. However, some attention must be paid to the student's writing. There must be a level of accountability for engaging in critical thought. That accountability can be provided through teacher observation, discussion, peer review, self-assessment, the use of a rubric (see an example below), or any number of other ways, including an actual grade. If students begin to realize that there is no check for understanding or accountability for their critical writing, all but the most motivated students will quickly lose interest and the critical element of the writing will all but evaporate.

Sample Rubric: Student Assessment of Critical Writing

Category	1	2	3	Points
Presentation of Topic	The topic is unclear.	The topic is evident.	The topic is presented clearly.	
Supporting Information	Supporting information is not evident or is unrelated to the topic.	Supporting information is evident, but limited.	Supporting information clarifies or enriches the topic.	
Organization	There is little to no organization.	The organization is difficult to follow.	The organization is easy to follow.	
Understanding	I'm uncomfortable with my understanding of the topic.	I'm comfortable with my understanding of the topic.	I'm confident with my understanding of the topic.	
			Total:	

Natural Closing Product

Finally, as many teachers have realized (and the authors recommend), a short critical writing exercise can serve as an excellent closing product for the lesson frame (Fundamental Five practice number one, Frame the Lesson). As the closing product for the day's lesson, a trainer working with a group of teachers could provide a writing prompt similar to the following:

"I will answer the following question: what obstacles might I have to overcome to implement the Fundamental Five in my classroom?"

In less than five minutes, this question could be answered on a three-by-five-inch index card, and the teachers could hand the card to the trainer as they exit the training room. With this critical writing activity, the rigor level of the instruction is increased to the analysis level, and relevance is increased as the teacher considers how he or she will personally overcome the obstacles that may arise as he or she attempts to apply what was learned in a different setting. In addition, with a quick scan of the cards, the trainer can determine the general level of understanding of the lesson for the group as a whole as well as for individual participants. This determination then assists the trainer in planning the activities for the next training session. This is the very definition of quality, proactive instruction.

CHAPTER EIGHT

New Beginnings

Though there is no question that the five practices presented in this book are not new, the better understanding of their individual power and the discovery of their power when implemented as a cohesive unit represents a new beginning for effective instruction. Instead of waiting for the next new program, or fearing the encroachment of increasing accountability standards coupled with increasing class size and decreasing resources, teachers have at their disposal the skill set to have their students exceed expectations on a consistent basis. E. Don Brown (personal communication, June 2010), a former president of the National Association of Secondary School Principals and one of the architects of *Breaking Ranks* (1996), believes that if teachers would harness the power that the Fundamental Five provides them in the classroom, many of the problems that they face in terms of student motivation, behavior, and academic performance would quickly become areas of strength.

This might seem to be an endorsement that borders on hyperbole, until one sees the data from campuses that have adopted the Fundamental Five as a core instructional framework. Below is just a small sample of the early performance data that is being collected. Do know that the authors are not claiming that the Fundamental Five is the only reason for the changes in the data. However, on all of the campuses presented below, the most significant change between the first set of collected data and the second set of collected data is Fundamental Five staff training coupled with a focus on increasing the frequency of the use of the Fundamental Five practices in the classroom.

Early Performance Data

Hairgrove Elementary School is an urban campus in Houston, Texas. The campus serves approximately 925 students in grades prekindergarten (PK) to five. Critical demographic information is listed in the chart below (as of 2010).

Student Group	Percentage of Student Population
African American	8.3%
Hispanic	78.3%
White	9.8%
Native American	0.0%
Asian / Pacific Islander	3.5%
Economically Disadvantaged	79.8%
Limited English Proficient	49.8%

The overall passing rates for Hairgrove Elementary students on the annual state accountability test (TAKS) before and after the staff were trained on the use of the Fundamental Five practices of effective instruction are listed in the chart below.

Tested Subject	2009 Passing Rate	2010 Passing Rate	Change
Reading	90%	93%	+3
Writing	92%	93%	+1
Mathematics	93%	98%	+5
Science	86%	96%	+10

Lee Elementary School is an urban campus in Houston, Texas. The campus serves approximately 1,175 students in grades PK to five. Critical demographic information is listed in the chart below (as of 2010).

Student Group	Percentage of Student Population
African American	7.6%
Hispanic	57.6%
White	14.2%
Native American	0.3%
Asian / Pacific Islander	20.3%
Economically Disadvantaged	60.5%
Limited English Proficient	48.2%

The overall passing rates for Lee Elementary students on the annual state accountability test (TAKS) before and after the staff were trained on the use of the Fundamental Five practices of effective instruction are listed in the chart below.

Tested Subject	2009 Passing Rate	2010 Passing Rate	Change
Reading	88%	92%	+4
Writing	92%	95%	+3
Mathematics	93%	97%	+4
Science	91%	95%	+4

In the late spring of 2010, Midland Independent School District, a large urban district in Texas, decided that the staff of its four junior high schools and two freshman schools would be trained on the use of the Fundamental Five instructional practices beginning in the 2010 fall semester. Critical district demographic information is listed in the chart below (as of 2010).

Student Group	Percentage of Student Population
African American	9.4%
Hispanic	54.8%
White	34.3%
Native American	0.4%
Asian / Pacific Islander	1.1%
Economically Disadvantaged	52.9%
Limited English Proficient	9.0%

To gauge the effectiveness of the staff training, baseline classroom observation data was collected through the use of the PowerWalks instructional observation system during April and May 2010. Teachers and administrators received training on the Fundamental Five practices during the months of September and October 2010. Classroom observation data from the month of November 2010 were collected to determine the effect of the Fundamental Five training on teacher practice. The graph below shows the change in the frequency of observed use of the Fundamental Five practices in participating secondary school classrooms.

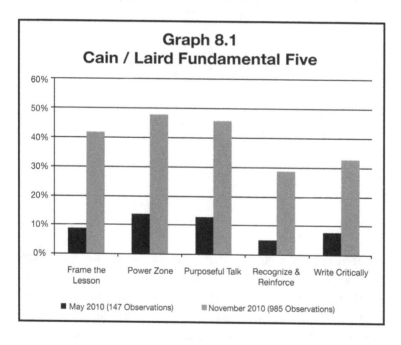

In addition to the collection of data on the use of the Fundamental Five instructional practices, data were collected on the rigor and relevance of the observed instruction. The graph below illustrates the change in observed rigor and relevance of typical instruction in secondary school classrooms.

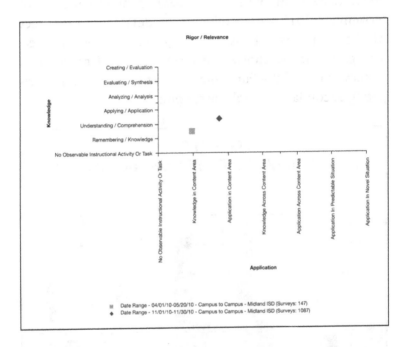

It must be stressed that correlation is not causation, meaning that there are other factors both visible and invisible that can also be driving the positive changes documented in the data above. But the dramatic and rapid improvement in both student performance and adult practice that is being observed in the field, at scale, in diverse and even adverse academic settings that followed the introduction of the Fundamental Five is exciting. The promise of better teaching and improved learning, which many naysayers seem to believe is empty, is in fact well within our means.

Leading and Lagging Indicators

As one embarks on the journey to implement the Fundamental Five on a campus or in a classroom, there will be difficulties that one will have to overcome, and at times, one could even begin to feel somewhat overwhelmed. This is not unusual; the changing of personal habits and practices is difficult. But one must push through the tough part. When looking at school improvement, it is the change in adult behavior that is the leading indicator. The change in student performance is the lagging indicator. It is the extended exposure to the improvements in adult practice that drives the improvement in student performance. If, by objective measure (for example, the data provided by PowerWalks), adult practice is improving, one can be confident that improved student academic performance will follow. The search for the next program in which to plug in "those" students is at best a short-term response, which only buys time to potentially solve the core problems. To actually solve the core problems of education requires the most adaptable, engaging, and creative tool at our disposal, *the classroom teacher*. It is the classroom teacher who focuses on the fundamentals, works at the fundamentals, and executes the fundamentals with increasing frequency and quality that will lead entire classrooms of students to the uncharted territory of sustained high-rigor/high-relevance instruction.

In closing, consider the effect that each of the Fundamental Five practices has in the classroom. Framing the lesson has a positive impact on instructional planning and delivery and improves student retention of the content. Working in the power zone improves both student discipline and on-task behavior. The use of frequent, small-group, purposeful talk about the learning can increase both the rigor and relevance of classroom instruction and improves student retention of the content. Recognition and reinforcement improve both student performance and student behavior. Writing critically increases the rigor and relevance of classroom instruction, improves student retention of the content, and improves student literacy skills. Executed as a cohesive unit, the Fundamental Five improves the quality of classroom instruction, improves student behavior, and improves student retention of the presented material. All that is required to successfully implement these five practices is teacher awareness and teacher willingness to improve.

Think. Work. Achieve.

CHAPTER NINE

Encore

When the authors present to large groups, a question that is frequently asked is, "So how do you really do this in a given class?"

In response to that question, the authors share "The Big Easy's Secret Plan for Stress-Free Instruction," which was scripted by Dr. Jim Davis and is presented below.

Prior to the class, the teacher should:

1. Preview the scope and sequence.
2. Frame the Lesson (FRAME THE LESSON).
   a. Today, we will…
   b. I will write… (WRITE CRITICALLY).
3. Plan or select one mid-to-high rigor question to ask the students (FREQUENT, SMALL-GROUP, PURPOSEFUL TALK ABOUT THE LEARNING).

During the class, the teacher should:

1. Greet the students at the classroom door, welcome them to class, and shake their hands (RECOGNIZE AND REINFORCE).
2. Read the lesson frame to the class (FRAME THE LESSON).
3. Move to the power zone and start the lesson (WORK IN THE POWER ZONE).
4. At a point near the middle of the class period, stop. Have the students turn to their neighbor. Ask the students to discuss the mid-to-high rigor question that was preselected. Let the students talk in their small group for two minutes (FREQUENT, SMALL-GROUP, PURPOSEFUL TALK ABOUT THE LEARNING).
5. Remain in the power zone and monitor the students' conversations (WORK IN THE POWER ZONE; FREQUENT, SMALL-GROUP, PURPOSEFUL TALK ABOUT THE LEARNING; and additional opportunities to RECOGNIZE AND REINFORCE).
6. Cue the students to conclude their conversation.
7. Compliment the students on their effort and behavior. If a student made a really good point in his or her discussion, have the student share the discussion point with the class (RECOGNIZE AND REINFORCE).
8. Have the students continue with the planned instruction and activities. While the students are working, wander through the room checking the progress of individual students (WORK IN THE POWER ZONE, continue to RECOGNIZE AND REINFORCE).
9. With five minutes left in the class period, give the students an index card or Post-it note. Have the

students answer the closing question in three to six sentences (WRITE CRITICALLY and FRAME THE LESSON).

10. Collect the index cards or Post-it notes at the door, as the students exit the class.

After the class, the teacher should:

1. Scan the written responses.
2. Use the information from the students' writing to create the warm-up activity for the next time the class meets.

As one can see, "The Big Easy's Secret Plan for Stress-Free Instruction" provides structure to the class period and embeds all five fundamental instructional practices within almost any activity the teacher may have planned, in a non-intrusive and authentic fashion.

Stories from the Field

One of the authors, Sean Cain, was conducting Fundamental Five training on a campus with a number of experienced staff members. The training was spread out over a number of weeks with teachers receiving training, then working to implement the training, then debriefing on the experience before adding on more of the practices. Session after session, one veteran teacher in particular was seemingly not interested in anything that Cain had to say. But being a professional, she would sit quietly and go back to her classroom and give a cursory attempt to implement the practice that was presented. On the day of the last training session, as Cain was walking out the door, he passed the "tough, seen it all more than once" teacher, and she said, *"Cain, don't tell my principal because I'll never hear the end of it, but this stuff really works."*

What better endorsement could one receive?

References

Allen, R. H. 2010. *High-Impact Teaching Strategies for the 'XYZ' Era of Education*. Boston, MA: Allyn and Bacon.

Anderson, et al. 2001. *A Taxonomy for Learning, Teaching, and Assessing: A Revision of Bloom's Taxonomy of Educational Objectives*. New York, NY: Longman.

Berliner, B. 1990. *Alternatives to School District Consolidation*. Knowledge Brief Number Two, Far West Laboratory. (ERIC Document Reproduction Service No, ED 322 621).

Bloom, B. S. 1956. *Taxonomy of Educational Objectives (Cognitive Domain)*. New York, NY: Longman.

Breaking Ranks: Changing an American Intuition. 1996. Reston, VA: A Report of the National Association of Secondary School Principals on the High School of the 21st Century.

Brown, E. 2010. Personal communication with authors. Houston, Texas.

Cain, S. 2009. The State of Current Instructional Practices in Selected Schools in the State of Texas. Unpublished Research.

Cain, S., and M. Laird. 2010. The Impact of the Fundamental Five Practices of Effective Instruction on Student

Achievement in Selected Schools in the State of Texas. Unpublished Research.

Ericson, H. L. 2002. *Concept-Based Curriculum and Instruction: Teaching Beyond the Facts.* Thousand Oaks, CA: Corwin Press.

Kotulak, R. 1997. *Inside the Brain.* Kansas City, KS: Andrews McMeel Publishing.

Marzano, R. L., D. J. Pickering, and J. E. Pollock. 2001. *Classroom Instruction That Works: Research-Based Strategies for Increasing Student Achievement.* Alexandria, VA: Association for Supervision and Curriculum Development.

McCollough, A. W., and E. K. Vogel. 2008. *Scientific American Mind* (June), http://www.cogmed.com/working-memory-they-found-your-brain's-spam-filter.

O'Hare, W. 1988. *The Rise of Poverty in Rural America.* Washington, DC: Population Reference Bureau ERIC. (ERIC Document Reproduction Service No RC 016 865).

Paul, R., and L. Elder. 2006. *The International Critical Thinking, Reading & Writing Test: How to Assess Close Reading and Substantive Writing.* Dillon Beach, CA: The Foundation for Critical Thinking Press.

Paul, R., and L. Elder. 2007. *The Thinker's Guide to How to Write a Paragraph: The Art of Substantive Writing.* Dillon Beach, CA: The Foundation for Critical Thinking Press.

Pfeffer, P., and R. Sutton. 2000. *The Knowing Doing Gap: How Smart Companies Turn Knowledge into Action.* Boston, MA: Harvard Business School Press.

Schmoker, M. 2006. *Results Now: How We Can Achieve Unprecedented Improvements in Teaching and Learning.*

Alexandria, VA: Association for Supervision and Curriculum Development.

Snowman, J., and R. Biehler. 2006. *Psychology Applied to Teaching*. Boston, MA: Houghton Mifflin Company.

Sousa, D. A. 2001. *How the Brain Learns*. Thousand Oaks, CA: Corwin Press.

Walberg, H. J., and W. J. Fowler. 1986. *Expenditure and Size Efficiencies of Public School Districts*. New Jersey Department of Education. (ERIC Document Reproduction Service No, ED 274 471).

About the Authors

Sean Cain spent the formative years of his career working in difficult instructional settings. Recognized for the success of both his students and the systems he designed and implemented, he quickly moved up through the instructional leadership ranks. This culminated in his last public education position as State Director of Innovative School Redesign (Texas).

Currently, Cain serves as the Chief Idea Officer for Lead Your School (LYS), a confederation of successful school leaders dedicated to improving student, campus, and district performance. A passionate speaker, Cain is a sought-after national presenter and trains educators in schools and districts across the county. The primary foci of Cain's current research and fieldwork are making complex problems solvable and the translation of theory into systematic practice. You can follow the progress of Cain and the educators he works with through his daily online column at www. LYSNation.com and read his daily observations at www. Twitter.com/LYSNation.

Mike Laird is currently a public school administrator as well as an adjunct professor, who mentors aspiring school leaders.

Along with his continuing service to public education as a teacher, coach, assistant principal, principal, and assistant superintendent, he proudly served his country for twenty-two years as an officer in the United States Army Reserve.

Dr. Laird is a well-respected presenter at both the local and national levels and continues to present at conferences, such as the National Association of Secondary School Principals and the American Association of School Administrators. His current focus is on the leadership and methods necessary to "rapidly" improve the academic performance of students in today's high stakes accountability environment.

Praise for the Fundamental Five

"Purposeful discussion and positive emotions are vital to supporting educational achievement. I loudly applaud the authors in offering teachers *practical* advice as to how this can be achieved in their classroom."

—Dr. Rich Allen, author, international speaker and trainer

"*The Fundamental Five: The Formula for Quality Instruction* is more than a theoretical treatise, and it is certainly not a book that re-covers the well traveled paths so often used as talking points in public education. Solidly anchoring one corner of Cain's Foundation Trinity, the Fundamental Five has the power and 'how-to' tone that can transform America's schools."

—Dr. Michael Seabolt, High School Principal

CPSIA information can be obtained
at www.ICGtesting.com
Printed in the USA
LVHW011533250819
628854LV00005BA/62